THE RESILIENT SECTOR
REVISITED

THE RESILIENT SECTOR REVISITED

THE NEW CHALLENGE TO NONPROFIT AMERICA

Second Edition

LESTER M. SALAMON

With the assistance of
S. WOJCIECH SOKOLOWSKI

BROOKINGS INSTITUTION PRESS
Washington, D.C.

THE BROOKINGS INSTITUTION
1775 Massachusetts Avenue, N.W., Washington, D.C. 20036
www.brookings.edu
The Brookings Institution is a private nonprofit organization devoted to research, education, and publication on important issues of domestic and foreign
policy. Its principal purpose is to bring the highest quality independent research
and analysis to bear on current and emerging policy problems. Interpretations
or conclusions in Brookings publications should be understood to be solely those
of the authors.

Library of Congress Cataloging-in-Publication data

Salamon, Lester M.
    [Resilient sector]
    The resilient sector revisited : the new challenge to nonprofit America /
Lester M. Salamon ; with the assistance of S. Wojciech Sokolowski. — Second
edition.
        pages   cm
    Earlier edition published in 2003 as: The resilient sector : the state of nonprofit
America.
    Includes bibliographical references and index.
    ISBN 978-0-8157-2425-4 (pbk. : alk. paper) — ISBN 978-0-8157-2426-1
(ebook : alk. paper)
    1. Nonprofit organizations—United States.   I. Title.
    HD2769.2.U6S246 2015
    338.7'4—dc23
                                                                2015019157

9 8 7 6 5 4 3 2 1

Printed on acid-free paper

Typeset in Adobe Garamond

Composition by Westchester Publishing Services

To the unsung heroes
who operate and manage America's nonprofit organizations,
a truly resourceful and dedicated band of social entrepreneurs
who deserve our full gratitude and respect

Contents

Preface and Acknowledgments

This book is an updated version of the introduction to a much longer book entitled *The State of Nonprofit America,* first published in 2002 and issued in a fully revised second edition in 2012.

The objective of this longer book, as I noted in the preface to the second edition, was to rescue the nonprofit sector from the dilemma arising from the fact that the recent flurry of academic and policy attention to this important set of institutions "has not yet generated the clear understanding that is needed of the sector's changing position and role. For one thing, nonprofit organizations continue to be caught up in the longstanding political conflict over the relative roles of the state and the market in responding to public problems, creating a heavy ideological overlay that distorts our view and systematically blocks out uncomfortable facts. Beyond this, the sheer outpouring of information creates its own confusion. Once starved for information, nonprofit practitioners are now deluged by it. Fitting the bits and pieces together into an integrated understanding thus becomes a full-time occupation, something that few harried practitioners or volunteer board members have the luxury to pursue."

In addition, the information resources available on this sector, though improving, remain grossly imperfect, creating enormous traps for unsuspecting observers. To cite just two of these traps, widely published data on charitable giving contain enormous amounts of double-counting, and the official forms on which nonprofits report annually on their sources of income merge most government funding together with private fees and charges in a category called "program service revenue," thereby grossly obscuring the true scale of the immense government funding flowing to this sector.

The project out of which this volume emerged was conceived as a response to this dilemma. It sought to provide a comprehensive, but readable, assessment of the state of America's nonprofit sector at what turns out to be a pivotal moment in its development. More than a compilation of facts and figures, the original book sought to interpret what is going on and make it understandable to the broad cross section of informed opinion on which the future of this sector ultimately rests.

Inevitably, this was no mean undertaking. Nonprofit organizations are almost infinitely varied. They come in different sizes, operate in widely different fields, perform different functions, and support themselves in varied ways. What is more, all of these features are in flux. To do justice to this variety and dynamism, the earlier volume grew into a 708-page edited book, with chapters on each of the components of the nonprofit sector and on a set of important crosscutting issues.

This larger book has filled an important niche in the academic study and teaching on the nonprofit sector both in the United States and abroad. From the outset, however, it was clear that policymakers, practitioners, board members, and academics teaching courses in which the nonprofit sector is an important component but not the only focus needed a more succinct, interpretive overview, preferably available in a stand-alone volume in addition to serving as a useful introduction to the larger work. Fortunately, Brookings Institution Press was amenable to issuing the introduction to the larger volume as a separate book entitled *The Resilient Sector: The State of Nonprofit America* (2003). And now, with the present volume, the press has given me an opportunity to provide a wider audience with an updated version of the introduction to the second edition of the larger volume, taking the story of the evolution of America's nonprofit sector well into the post–2008 financial crisis period. As will become clear, many of the trends, and many of the dangers, evident in the original introduction to the second edition of the larger volume have intensified in the period following its publication in 2012, making the earlier call for a process of renewal for the nonprofit sector issued there all the more urgent.

As before, I want to acknowledge the substantial debt of gratitude I owe to the extraordinary group of colleagues who worked with me over several years to produce the updated portrait of America's nonprofit sector and its component parts that was published as the second edition of *The State of Nonprofit America*. Without the factually grounded and carefully interpreted chapters that form the core of this longer book, the present shorter overview would never have been possible. Enormous thanks are also due to Dr. S. Wojciech Sokolowski, whose mastery of the complex data sources available on the nonprofit sector in the United States, and the considerable conceptual and empirical traps with which they are littered, made it possible to provide a much clearer picture of the realities under way than has generally been available. My thanks go out as well to Janet Walker at the Brookings Institution Press, whose persistence played a big part in making it possible for this project to cross the finish line, and to colleagues Chelsea Newhouse and Stephanie Geller at Johns Hopkins for production assistance and for help in generating the timely insights into the challenges facing nonprofit agencies at the ground level that have emerged from our Nonprofit Listening Post Project and that add an extra element of verification to the observations made throughout this volume.

Needless to say, however, the opinions and interpretations offered here are my responsibility alone, and may not represent the views of any of the authors of the full *State of Nonprofit America* volume or of any organizations with which I may be affiliated or that have supported or published the work. What is more, although I have attempted to bring the story of America's nonprofit sector up to the present, inevitably it has not been possible to make this account as current as yesterday's newspaper. Far from diminishing the value of this book, however, it is my hope that these shifts make it clear why the kind of interpretive perspective offered here is so useful. Readers can judge for themselves whether the trends and developments I have highlighted are the ones that will prevail in the years immediately ahead. If the account here provides a checklist against which to judge emerging realities, and a spur to actions that resolve challenges I have identified, it will have served its purpose well.

Finally, this book is dedicated to the incredibly resourceful and dedicated, but far too unsung, men and women who manage and operate America's amazing nonprofit sector. To them we owe an enormous debt of gratitude for nurturing and shepherding a set of institutions that not only delivers critical services but also embodies and sustains a value that is crucial to the American character, the value of individual initiative for the common good. Without them we would all be much worse off.

Annapolis, Maryland
May 4, 2015

1

Introduction

A struggle is under way for the "soul" of America's nonprofit sector, that vast collection of private, tax-exempt hospitals, higher-education institutions, day care centers, nursing homes, symphonies, social service agencies, environmental organizations, civil rights organizations, and dozens of others that make up this important, but poorly understood, component of American life.

This is not a wholly new struggle, to be sure. From earliest times nonprofits have been what sociologists refer to as "dual identity," or even "conflicting multiple identity," organizations.[1] They are not-for-profit organizations required to operate in a profit-oriented market economy. They draw heavily on voluntary contributions of time and money, yet are expected to meet professional standards of performance and efficiency. They are part of the private sector, yet serve important public purposes.

In recent years, however, these identities have grown increasingly varied and increasingly difficult to bridge, both in the public's mind and in the day-to-day operations of individual organizations. In a sense, America's

Figure 1-1.   *Four Impulses Shaping the Future of Nonprofit America*

nonprofit organizations seem caught in a force field, buffeted by a variety of impulses, four of which seem especially significant. For the sake of simplicity I label these *voluntarism, professionalism, civic activism*, and *commercialism*, as shown in figure 1-1, though in practice each is a more complex bundle of pressures.

What makes these four impulses especially important is that their relative influence can profoundly affect the role that nonprofit organizations play and the way in which they operate. Understanding this force field and the factors shaping its dynamics thus becomes central to understanding the future both of particular organizations and of the nonprofit sector as a whole.

Sadly, far too little attention has been paid to the significant tensions among these impulses. The nonprofit sector has long been the hidden subcontinent on the social landscape of American life, regularly revered but rarely seriously scrutinized or understood. In part, this lack of scrutiny is due to the ideological prism through which these organizations are too often viewed. Indeed, a lively ideological contest has long raged over the extent to which we can rely on nonprofit institutions to handle critical public needs, with conservatives focusing laser-like attention on the sector's strengths in order to fend off calls for greater reliance on government, and liberals often restricting their attention to its limitations in order to justify calls for expanded governmental protections.

Through it all, though largely unheralded—and perhaps unrecognized by either side—a classically American compromise has taken shape. This compromise was forged early in the nation's history, but it was broadened and solidified in the 1960s. Under it, nonprofit organizations in an ever-widening range of fields were made the beneficiaries of government support to provide a growing array of services—from health care to scientific research—that Americans wanted but were reluctant to have government provide directly.[2] More, perhaps, than any other single factor, this government-nonprofit partnership is responsible for the growth of the nonprofit sector as we know it today.

Since about 1980, however, that compromise has come under considerable assault. Conservative critics, concerned about what they see as an unholy alliance between the once-independent nonprofit sector and the state, have called for a return to the sector's supposed purely voluntary roots.[3] Liberal critics have bewailed the sector's departure from a more socially activist past and its surrender to professionalism.[4] At the same time, the country's nonprofit managers, facing an extraordinary range of other challenges as well—significant demographic shifts, fundamental changes in public policy and public attitudes, new accountability demands, massive technological developments, and changes in lifestyle, to cite just a few—have been left to their own devices and have turned increasingly to the market to survive. Through it all, nonprofit America has responded with considerable creativity to its many challenges, but the responses have pulled it in directions that are, at best, not well understood and, at worst, corrosive of the sector's special character and role.

Despite the significance of these developments, little headway has been made in tracking them systematically, in assessing the impact they are having both generally and for particular types of organizations, and in effectively getting the results into the hands of nonprofit managers, policymakers, the press, and the public at large. This book seeks to fill this gap, to offer a clear, up-to-date assessment of a set of institutions that we have long taken for granted but that the Frenchman Alexis de Tocqueville recognized over 175 years ago to be "more deserving of our attention" than any other part of the American experiment.[5] More specifically, the book makes available, in a more accessible form, an updated summary of a much larger inquiry into the state of America's nonprofit sector that the present author carried out with an extraordinary team of collaborators and that was published in a prior volume.[6]

Perhaps the central theme that emerged from this larger project, and that is a central theme of this book, is the theme of *resilience,* of a set of institutions and traditions facing not only enormous challenges but also important opportunities and finding ways to respond to both with considerable creativity and resolve. Indeed, nonprofit America appears to be well along in a fundamental process of reengineering that calls to mind the similar transformation that large segments of America's business sector have been undergoing since the late 1980s.[7] Faced with an increasingly competitive environment, nonprofit organizations have been called on to make fundamental changes in the way they operate. And that is just what they have been doing.

The problem, however, is that, although the sector's organizations have been responding resiliently, those responses are taking a toll on their ability to perform some of their most important functions. As a consequence, nonprofit America is ironically endangered by its own resilience. In a sense, nonprofits have been forced to choose between two competing imperatives: a *survival imperative* and a *distinctiveness imperative,* between the things they need to do to survive in an increasingly demanding market environment and the things they need to do to retain their distinctiveness and basic character.[8] In recent years, the survival imperative seems to have gained the upper hand. The question for the future is whether it will continue to do so, or whether the nation's nonprofit sector will find better ways to balance these demands, and how much understanding and help they will receive from the broader society to allow them to do so.

Any account of the future of nonprofit America must therefore be a story in three parts, focusing, first, on the challenges and opportunities that America's nonprofit sector is confronting, then examining how the sector's institutions are responding to these challenges and opportunities, and finally assessing the consequences of these responses both for individual organizations and subsectors and for nonprofit America as a whole. Against this backdrop, it will then be possible to identify some of the steps that might be needed to help America's nonprofit organizations evade the dangers they face.

The balance of this volume offers such an account. To set the stage for it, however, it may be useful to remind readers what the nonprofit sector is and why it is so deserving of our attention. It is to this task that we therefore turn in the next chapter.

2

The Stakes:
What Is the Nonprofit Sector
and Why Do We Need It?

The nonprofit sector is one of the most important components of American life, but it is also one of the least understood. Few people are even aware of this sector's existence, though most have some contact with it at some point in their lives. Included within this sector are most of the nation's premier hospitals and universities; almost all of its orchestras and opera companies; a significant share of its theater companies; all of its religious congregations; the bulk of its environmental advocacy and civil rights organizations; huge numbers of its family service, children's service, neighborhood development, antipoverty, and community health agencies; not to mention its professional associations, labor unions, and social clubs. Also included are the numerous support organizations, such as foundations and community chests, which help to generate financial assistance for these organizations and to encourage the traditions of giving, volunteering, and service that undergird them.

More formally, the nonprofit sector consists of a broad range of private organizations that are generally exempted from federal, as well as state and local, taxation on the grounds that they serve some public purpose.[1] The term *nonprofit,* which is commonly used to depict these organizations and which will be used here, is actually a misnomer: these organizations are permitted to earn profits—that is, end up with an excess of income over expenditures in a given year; what is prohibited is the distribution of any such profit to organizational directors or managers. Technically, then, we might more accurately refer to these organizations as *nonprofit-distributing* organizations.

Within this complex array of organizations are two broad types: first, *member-serving organizations,* such as labor unions, business associations, social clubs, and fraternal societies; and second, *public-serving organizations,* such as hospitals, universities, social service agencies, and cultural venues. For the purpose of this volume, we focus exclusively on the second type, the public-serving organizations, which make up by far the largest, and most visible, component of the tax-exempt organization sector. Also known as charitable organizations, most of these organizations earn their exemption from federal income taxation under section 501(c)(3) of the Internal Revenue Code, which is reserved for organizations that operate "exclusively for religious, charitable, scientific, or educational purposes." Alone among tax-exempt organizations, the 501(c)(3) organizations are eligible to receive tax-deductible donations from individuals and businesses, that is, gifts that the individuals and businesses can deduct from their income when computing their income taxes. This reflects the fact that the recipient organizations are expected to serve broad public purposes, not just the interests and needs of the organizations' members. The public-serving component of the nonprofit sector also includes another set of organizations, however, that are eligible for tax exemption under section 501(c)(4) of the Internal Revenue Code, which is reserved for so-called social welfare organizations. The major difference between 501(c)(4) and 501(c)(3) organizations is that the former are permitted to engage in lobbying without limit, whereas the latter have limits on the extent of their lobbying activity. Because of this, however, contributions made to 501(c)(4) organizations are not tax deductible.[2]

Size of the Sector

No one knows for sure how many tax-exempt nonprofit organizations exist in the United States, since large portions of the sector are essentially unincorporated and the data available on even the formal organizations are notoriously imperfect. A conservative estimate would put the number of formally constituted tax-exempt organizations, as of 2014, at just over 1.7 million, of which just over 1.3 million are in the public-serving component of the sector, and the remaining 400,000 in the member-serving component.[3]

Within this public-serving portion of the entire tax-exempt universe, moreover, are four subgroups of organizations:

—approximately 700,000 service and expressive organizations, ranging from hospitals to advocacy organizations and cultural institutions;
—a little over 81,000 501(c)(4) social welfare and lobbying organizations;
—approximately 140,000 foundations, federated funders, and other funding intermediaries; and
—over 400,000 religious congregations.

As of 2011 these public-serving nonprofit organizations employed close to 11.4 million paid workers. This represents 10 percent of the entire U.S. labor force and makes the nonprofit paid workforce the third largest of any U.S. industry, behind only retail trade and manufacturing but ahead of such industries as construction, finance and insurance, and transportation (see figure 2-1). With volunteers included, and their volunteer time translated into the equivalent number of full-time workers, the workforce of nonprofit, public-benefit organizations swells by another 4.5 million full-time-equivalent workers, making it the largest workforce of any U.S. industry—larger than construction, larger than finance and insurance, even larger than retail trade and all the branches of manufacturing combined, as figure 2-1 also shows.[4]

Employment provides just one measure of the scale of America's public-serving nonprofit organizations. Also impressive are the financial

Figure 2-1.   *Nonprofit Employment vs. Employment in Other U.S. Industries, 2012*

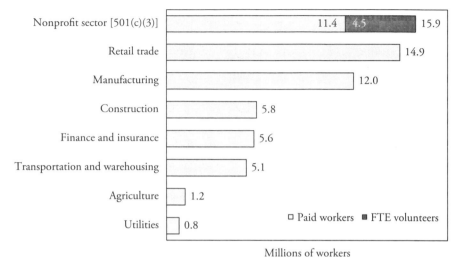

Millions of workers

Source: Bureau of Labor Statistics, Quarterly Census of Employment and Wages; U.S. Census Bureau, September Supplement to the Current Population Survey. See chapter 2, note 4.

resources that these organizations command. As of 2011 the revenue of public-serving, nonprofit organizations stood at just under $1.8 trillion. Most (86 percent) of this revenue, a sizable $1.539 trillion, accrued to the service and expressive organizations, which form the economic core of the sector and also the core of its service and expressive functions. The balance went to the funding intermediaries ($100 billion), religious congregations ($65 billion), and 501(c)(4) social welfare agencies ($85 billion).[5]

Among the service and expressive organizations, most of the revenue flows to health-related organizations. With 12 percent of the reporting organizations, this field captured 59 percent of all nonprofit service and expressive organization revenue in 2011, as shown in figure 2-2. Education and research organizations make up the second-largest component in terms of revenue, with 21 percent of the total. By contrast, social service providers, although the most numerous of the service and expressive organizations with 38 percent of the reporting organizations, accounted

Figure 2-2.   *Reporting Nonprofit Service and Expressive Organizations, Share of Organizations vs. Revenues, 2011*

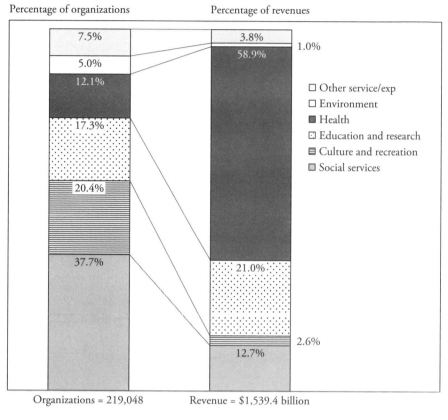

Percentage of organizations   Percentage of revenues

Organizations = 219,048   Revenue = $1,539.4 billion

Source: See chapter 2, note 5.

for a considerably smaller 13 percent of the revenue (though this was still a substantial nearly $200 billion).

These large categories disguise the huge array of separate services and activities in which nonprofit organizations are involved, however. A classification system developed by the National Center for Charitable Statistics, for example, identifies twenty-six major fields of nonprofit activity, and sixteen functions, from accreditation to fundraising, in each. Each major field is then further divided into subfields. Thus, for example, the field of arts, culture, and humanities has fifty-six subfields, and the field of education, forty-one. Altogether, this translates into close to a thousand different types of nonprofit organizations.[6]

Even this fails to do justice to the considerable diversity of the nonprofit sector. Although most of the employment and economic resources of this sector are concentrated in the sector's large organizations, most of the organizations are quite small, with few or no full-time employees. For example, in 2011, of the approximately 735,000 service and expressive organizations registered on the Internal Revenue Service's revised Exempt Organization Master File and considered still active, only 250,066, or about one-third, submitted the Form 990 required of all organizations with expenditures of $25,000 or more. The remaining two-thirds of the organizations are thus either delinquent or below the $25,000 spending threshold for filing.[7] Even among the filers, nearly half reported less than $100,000 in expenditures, and 75 percent reported less than $500,000 as of 2009. Taken together, these small organizations accounted for a mere 2.6 percent of the sector's total expenditures. By contrast, only about 4 percent of the organizations fell into the largest category ($10 million or more in expenditures), but these organizations accounted for nearly 83 percent of the sector's reported expenditures.[8] The overwhelming majority of the sector's organizations therefore account for only a tiny fraction of the sector's activity.

Revenue Sources

While most of its organizations are small, America's nonprofit sector is still a major economic presence, with over $1.5 trillion in revenues, as we have seen, just in its core service and expressive organizations. Where does this revenue come from?

According to popular mythology, the sector is mostly supported by private philanthropy. In reality, however, the revenue structure of the nonprofit sector differs strikingly from this popular conception, as shown in figure 2-3. In particular, the major source of revenue of nonprofit service and expressive organizations is fees and charges paid by their clients

Figure 2-3. *Nonprofit Service and Expressive Organization Revenue by Source, 2011*

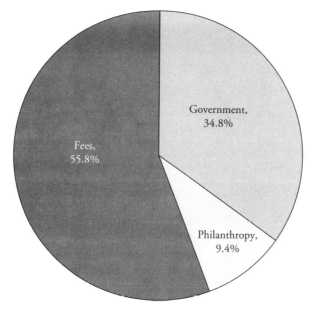

Source: See chapter 2, note 9.

or customers or their private insurers. This source alone accounted for 56 percent of nonprofit service and expressive organization revenue as of 2011.[9] Nor was philanthropy the second major source of revenue. Rather, that position was filled by government, which accounted for another 35 percent of overall service and expressive organization revenue. Philanthropy from all sources—individuals, foundations, and corporations—came in third among nonprofit revenue sources, accounting for only 9 percent of the total.

To be sure, philanthropy plays a more substantial role in some parts of the sector than in others. In particular, it is far more important in the expressive fields (arts and recreation) and civic affairs, where it accounts for 36 and 48 percent of the revenue, respectively. Even in the field of social services, long considered a major destination of charitable support, philanthropy's lead revenue role has been substantially eclipsed by both fees and government support.

Roles and Functions

Quite apart from their economic importance, nonprofit organizations perform major functions in national and community life, functions that define the stakes that the nation has in these institutions. Five such functions in particular deserve mention.

The Service Function

In the first place, nonprofit organizations are service providers: they deliver much of the hospital care, higher education, social services, cultural entertainment, employment and training, low-income housing, community development, and emergency aid available in this country. More concretely, these organizations constitute:

—half of the nation's hospitals;
—nearly a third of its private clinics and home health facilities;
—nearly one out of five of its nursing homes;
—close to 40 percent of its higher education institutions;
—70 percent of its individual and family service agencies;
—nearly 80 percent of its vocational rehabilitation facilities;
—30 percent of its day care centers;
—over 90 percent of its orchestras and operas; and
—the delivery vehicles for a major share of its foreign disaster assistance.

While disagreements exist over how "distinctive" nonprofit services are compared to those provided by businesses or governments, nonprofits are well known for identifying and addressing unmet needs, for innovating, and for delivering services of exceptionally high quality. It was thus nonprofit organizations that pioneered assistance to AIDS victims, hospice care, emergency shelter for the homeless, food pantries for the hungry, drug abuse treatment efforts, and dozens more too numerous to mention. Similarly, many of the premier educational and cultural institutions in the nation are private, nonprofit organizations—institutions such as Harvard, Princeton, Johns Hopkins, the Metropolitan Museum of Art, and the Cleveland Orchestra, to name just a few. To be sure, public and for-profit organizations also provide crucial services, but the country's hundreds of thousands of private, nonprofit groups add an extra dimension in meeting public needs, often responding to needs that neither the market nor the government is adequately addressing.

The Advocacy Function

In addition to delivering services, nonprofit organizations also contribute to national life by identifying unaddressed problems and bringing them to public attention, by protecting basic human rights, and by giving voice to a wide assortment of social, political, environmental, ethnic, and community interests and concerns. Most of the social movements that have animated American life over the past century or more operated in and through the nonprofit sector. Included here are the antislavery, women's suffrage, populist, progressive, civil rights, environmental, antiwar, women's, gay rights, and conservative movements. The nonprofit sector thus operates as a critical social safety valve, permitting aggrieved groups to bring their concerns to broader public attention and to rally support to improve their circumstances. This advocacy function may, in fact, be as important to the nation's social health as the service functions the sector also performs.

The Expressive Function

Political and policy concerns are not the only ones to which the nonprofit sector gives expression. Rather, an enormous variety of other concerns—artistic, religious, cultural, ethnic, social, recreational, gender, occupational—also find expression through this sector. Opera companies, symphonies, soccer clubs, churches, synagogues, fraternal societies, book clubs, and Girl Scouts are just some of the manifestations of this expressive function. Through them nonprofit organizations enrich human existence and contribute to the social and cultural vitality of American life.

The Community-Building Function

Nonprofit organizations are also important in building what scholars call "social capital," those bonds of trust and reciprocity that seem to be prerequisites for a democratic polity and a market economy to function effectively.[10] Alexis de Tocqueville understood this point well nearly two hundred years ago when he noted in *Democracy in America* that "feelings and opinions are recruited, the heart is enlarged, and the human mind is developed, only by the reciprocal influence of men upon one another. . . . These influences are almost null in democratic countries; they must therefore be artificially created and this can only by accomplished by associations."[11] By establishing connections among individuals, involvement in associations teaches norms of cooperation that carry over into political and economic life.

The Value Guardian Function[12]

Finally, nonprofit organizations embody, and therefore help to nurture and sustain, a crucial national value that emphasizes individual initiative in the public good. As noted earlier, they thus give institutional expression to two seemingly contradictory principles, both important parts of American national character: the principle of individualism, the notion that people should have the freedom to take the initiative on matters that concern them; and the principle of solidarity, the notion that people have responsibilities not only to themselves, but also to their fellow human beings and to the communities of which they are part. By fusing these two principles, nonprofit organizations reinforce both, establishing an arena of action through which individuals can take the initiative not simply to promote their own well-being but also to advance the well-being of others. This is not simply an abstract function, moreover. It takes tangible form in the billions of dollars in private charitable gifts that nonprofit organizations help to generate from the American public annually and in the 15.8 billion hours of volunteer time they stimulate.

Conclusion

In short, America's stake in the viability of its nonprofit organizations is substantial. Nonprofit America is a significant economic force, providing jobs and income to millions of people and contributing, through their salaries, to the tax base and economic prosperity of their states and communities. Beyond that, however, these organizations deliver critical services, provide outlets for political expression, enrich the country's social and cultural life, promote norms of reciprocity, and contribute to the quality of national life in countless other ways as well.

3

Four Impulses Shaping the Future
of Nonprofit America

W hile the key nonprofit functions of delivering services, influencing policy, giving expression to multiple interests and views, building community, and guarding crucial values outlined in the previous
chapter continue to characterize the nonprofit sector, powerful forces are
at work challenging and reshaping a number of them. Indeed, as noted
earlier, the nonprofit sector appears caught in a difficult force field con-
trolled by four conflicting impulses—voluntarism, professionalism, civic
activism, and commercialism—that are pulling it in somewhat different
directions. These impulses have implications, moreover, for a broad swath
of nonprofit features, from the *roles* that nonprofits play and the *strategies*
they use to their *style* of operation, their principal *reference groups,* their
organizational structure, their *management style,* and their *resource base.*
The power of these impulses is hardly identical in all fields, or in all organizations even within fields, but there is enough commonality to the

impulses to warrant a general characterization of their major features as a prelude to examining the drivers that are supporting or retarding each.

Voluntarism

Perhaps the most fundamental of these impulses, and the one that has fixed itself most securely onto popular conceptions of the nonprofit sector, is the voluntaristic impulse. This impulse carries much of the distinctive value claim of the nonprofit sector—its function as the vehicle through which individuals give expression to a wide assortment of social, cultural, religious, and other values and exercise individual initiative for the common good. But in recent years the voluntaristic impulse has come to be associated with a more stridently ideological conception of this sector. Indeed, as historian Waldemar Nielsen has shown, a "simplistic folklore" has attached itself to the American belief system with regard to this impulse. According to this folklore, the sectors of American society, particularly the nonprofit sector, "are neatly separated and exist in a static, ideologically partitioned relationship to each other, always have been, and ideally always should be."[1] This has given rise, including particularly in conservative circles, to an ideal image of a nonprofit sector that eschews involvement with government; is mostly staffed by selfless volunteers, many of them religiously inspired; and is wholly, or nearly wholly, supported by charitable giving.[2]

Whether in its more ideological or its more balanced forms, this voluntaristic impulse continues to exert a strong gravitational pull on public perceptions of the nonprofit sector, if less so on the actual operations of the sector's organizations. More specifically, as summarized in table 3-1, the voluntaristic impulse has come to be associated with a nonprofit sector whose primary *role* is to express and inculcate values. While a wide assortment of values can find resonance with this impulse, in recent years an especially strong current has arisen from the religious right and has found expression in the faith-based charity movement. Adherents to this perspective tend to attribute a wide range of human problems to the absence or underdevelopment of appropriate normative values. The *strategies*

Table 3-1. *Implications of the Four Impulses for Key Features of Nonprofit Operations*

Feature	Four Impulses			
	Voluntarism	Professionalism	Civic Activism	Commercialism
1) Role/objectives	• Overcome value deficits • Transform individuals • Relieve suffering	• Overcome physical, educational, or psychological deficits • Offer treatment	• Change structures of power • Change basic policies	• Use market means for social ends • Efficiently address social needs
2) Strategy	• Inculcate values • Counseling, personal renewal • Self-help • Temporary material assistance	• Medical model • Deliver services • Establish services as rights	• Asset model • Advocacy strategy • Organize citizens/build leadership • Access media/elites	• Promote social entrepreneurs • Locate market niches • Pursue self-sustaining income • Measure results
3) Operating style	• Pastoral • Normative • Paternalistic • Particularistic • Holistic	• Programmatic • Technocratic • Therapeutic • Universalistic • Secular	• Participatory • Confrontational • Critical	• Entrepreneurial • Efficiency oriented • Profit focused • Measurement driven
4) Principal reference group(s)	• Donors/volunteers • Members	• Staff • Profession • Clients	• Citizens • Community assets	• Corporate donors • Customers • Entrepreneurs
5) Organizational structure	• Fluid • Ad hoc	• Hierarchic • Segmented	• Modular • Federated • Alliances	• Product focused • Networked • Flexible
6) Management style	• Informal • Volunteer dominant • Spiritual	• Bureaucratic • Professional rule-bound	• Consensual • Collaborative • Participatory	• Responsive • Bottom-line focused • Disciplined
7) Resource base	• Voluntarism • Individual philanthropy	• Government • Fees • Institutional philanthropy	• Philanthropy • Voluntarism • Government	• Venture philanthropy • Sales • Vouchers

of intervention associated with this impulse therefore often emphasize counseling and self-help, coupled with temporary material assistance until the needed value messages are internalized and absorbed.

The *style* of intervention emphasized in the voluntaristic impulse therefore tends to be pastoral, normative, nonprofessional, holistic, and at times paternalistic. The stakeholders or *reference groups* most closely associated with this impulse are often individual donors and volunteers, who serve as role models for the disadvantaged and whose religious faith and values of hard work and personal responsibility are to be transmitted to those lacking them. The *organizational structures* associated with the voluntaristic impulse tend to be fluid and ad hoc, and the *management style* flexible and informal, as befits a volunteer-based staffing pattern. Finally, the *resource* needs of organizations imbued with the voluntaristic impulse are different in both scale and kind from those of other types of organizations, relying much more heavily on volunteers and charitable contributions than fees or government support.[3]

Professionalism

While the folklore of voluntarism remains dominant in much of the belief system surrounding the American nonprofit sector, a second impulse has profoundly shaped the reality of nonprofit operations. This is the impulse of *professionalism*. By professionalism, I mean the emphasis on specialized, subject-matter knowledge gained through formal training and delivered by paid experts.[4]

Professionalism has had a profound effect on the nonprofit sector, strengthening its capacities in important respects but at least partially displacing the sector's voluntaristic character.[5] While many of these effects have been attributed to the sector's involvement with government, in truth professionalism has probably had as much impact on government as government has had on professionalism, since a push by professionals to establish government licensing or program-staffing requirements is one of the crucial steps in establishing a profession.[6] At the least, the rise of professionalism within the nonprofit sector clearly predated the expansion of government involvement in the fields in which nonprofits are active. The transformation of private hospitals from small community institutions addressing the primary-care needs of communities into large bureaucratic institutions dominated by professionally trained doctors took place between 1885 and 1915, decades before Medicare and Medicaid had even been contemplated.[7] So, too, the professionalization of social work and the rise of "case work" rather than community organizing and social reform as the primary social-work mode of intervention was well along by the turn of the twentieth century and firmly in place by 1920.[8] What is more, the engine for this change was private philanthropy (in the form of local community chests) rather than government, as the scientific charity movement sought to replace what was widely perceived to be the inadequacies of well-meaning volunteers with the "trained intelligence" of professionals.[9]

While government did not introduce the professional impulse into the nonprofit sector, it has certainly helped to nurture and sustain it, both by providing professions a mechanism through which to enforce professional standards in government-funded programs and by providing the funds needed to hire professional staff. In the process, it has helped push nonprofit organizations in directions quite different from those imparted by the voluntaristic impulse. While it shares with voluntarism a deficit model emphasizing individual shortcomings as the cause of human problems, professionalism emphasizes not normative shortcomings but social, educational, physical, and psychological ones. The *role* of the nonprofit sector in this view is thus to offer professional services to disadvantaged clients. "Not alms but a friend," the long-standing slogan of the voluntaristic Boston Associated Charities, thus came to be replaced in professional social-worker circles by the mantra, "Neither alms nor a friend, but a professional service."[10]

Professionalism's *strategy* thus relies on a medical model, treating beneficiaries essentially as "patients" needing some form of "treatment," whether physical, educational, or psychological. Unlike the pastoral and holistic *operating style* characteristic of the voluntaristic impulse, the professional style is thus therapeutic, technocratic, segmented, and secular. The principal *reference group* for the professional impulse is not donors or beneficiaries but professional staff and the profession itself. Consistent with these features, professionalism creates *organizational structures* that are hierarchic and segmented; uses a *management style* that tends toward the bureaucratic, formal, and rule-bound; and requires the more ample and reliable *resources* of government and fees for support.

Civic Activism

Far different from both the voluntaristic and professional impulses is a third impulse coursing through the nonprofit sector: the impulse of *civic activism*. According to this perspective, the real source of the social ills besetting significant segments of the American public does not lie in the values, or in the psychological or skill deficits, of disadvantaged individuals. Rather, it lies in the structures of social, economic, and political power that such individuals confront in the broader society and in the unequal access to opportunities that results. The solution to these social ills therefore does not depend on moral preachment by well-meaning volunteers or on treatments administered by trained professionals but on the mobilization of social and political pressure to alter the structures of power and correct the imbalances of opportunity.[11]

The settlement house movement of the late nineteenth and early twentieth centuries clearly embodied this approach. Although providing immediate services to residents of the neighborhoods in which they were located, the real focus of the settlements, according to their historian, was to "bring about social reform, thus alleviating the underlying causes of social problems."[12] Seventy-five years later, this perspective remained uppermost in the mind of the first president of Independent Sector, the national umbrella group for American nonprofit organizations, who referred to "efforts to influence public policy" as "the role society most depends on [the voluntary sector] to perform."[13]

Instead of expressing values and transforming individuals, the civic activism impulse thus sees the fundamental *role* of the nonprofit sector to be eliminating the need for services by changing the balance of power in society and opening channels of opportunity to a broader swath of the population. Unlike the deficit strategies embodied in both the voluntaristic and professional impulses, the civic activism impulse embodies an asset model, using a *strategy* that sees in the disadvantaged population an enormous resource that can be mobilized and organized to bring about significant societal change. The basic *operating style* favored in this impulse is thus at once participatory, empowering, and confrontational, bringing pressure to bear on the powers that be to establish worker rights and offer access to education and other services that those on the bottom of the economic pyramid are unable to secure through market means. The principal *reference groups* for advocates of this perspective are ordinary citizens and those in greatest need, plus, where available, the media, to amplify the voices of otherwise voiceless constituencies. To achieve its empowerment objectives, the civic activism impulse fosters a modular *organizational structure,* with multiple linked nodes of action and mobilization. Its *management style* is consensual, participatory, and, where possible, collaborative, building alliances wherever willing partners can be located. And its *resource base* tends to be engaged individuals and, paradoxically in recent decades, government support.

Commercialism/Managerialism

Finally, in the past several decades, a fourth impulse has burst upon the nonprofit scene, *commercialism*, and its next-of-kin, *managerialism*.[14] This impulse, too, has its distinctive features and its distinctive implications for the operation of nonprofit organizations, some of which are consistent with the other impulses, but others of which are clearly in tension with them. The *role* that the commercial impulse presses on the nonprofit sector is a service role, but one that emphasizes managerial efficiency, innovation, and cost containment—dimensions that run counter to professionalism's emphasis, first and foremost, on effectiveness. The *strategy* embodied in the commercial impulse is the injection of a different type of professionalism into the operation of nonprofit organizations, not the subject-matter professionalism of doctors, social workers, and educators, but the business-oriented skills of the managerial professional.

This includes the use of strategic planning, quantitative measurement of outcomes, identification of market niches, and heightened attention to operational efficiency.

The *operating style* emphasized by the commercial/managerial impulse is entrepreneurial and businesslike, efficiency oriented and measurement driven. The principal *reference group* for those espousing the commercial impulse consists of business leaders, entrepreneurs, and actual or potential beneficiaries of an agency's services, who are reconceptualized as "customers." The commercial/managerial impulse calls for *organizational structures* that are focused on individual "products" or "lines of business," with metrics that track each line of business separately and network structures that encourage coordination but allow considerable autonomy for "product managers." The *management style* consistent with this impulse emphasizes clear lines of authority and disciplined performance, which is achieved through regular measurement against preset targets and the flexibility to advance and dismiss staff on the basis of performance rather than professional credentials. In terms of its *resource base,* the commercial impulse drives its adherents to search out sustainable revenue streams that can attract private investment capital for start-up and expansion. This means fee income and government entitlement program support, particularly such support delivered through vouchers and other market-based, consumer-side subsidies.

Conclusion: Navigating the Force Field

To be sure, these brief descriptions cannot do justice to the nuances and complexities of these various impulses. They are presented here as heuristic devices to suggest some of the major pressures to which nonprofit organizations are being subjected. What is more, while the impulses are in some tension with each other, there are also clearly points of mutual reinforcement. For example, professionalization and the growth of nonprofit paid staff may not have displaced the nonprofit involvement in advocacy, though they may have changed its character in certain ways. Similarly, the emergence of social entrepreneurs and social ventures, while a manifestation of the commercial impulse, also reinforces the voluntaristic impulse emphasizing private initiative in the common good. The challenge, therefore, is not to find the single best impulse to follow but rather the combination that produces the most meaningful and appropriate balance needed to allow organizations to survive and grow while still holding true to their distinctive attributes.

These impulses are not, moreover, disembodied concepts floating in space. Rather, they take concrete form in the actions of the sector's stakeholders—those who provide the resources, set the regulations and incentives, serve on the boards, operate the organizations, frame public perceptions, and lend their support in countless other ways. Lacking the firm anchor of a single clear, dominant raison d'être—such as maximizing profit in the case of business and securing popular political support in the case of government—nonprofits are especially vulnerable to being pulled this way and that by whichever pressure is dominant at the moment.

And this is just what appears to be happening at the present time. Responding brilliantly and resiliently to a variety of dominant challenges and pressures, significant components of the nonprofit sector have moved far from the sweet spot that has historically earned the sector public trust, and too little attention has been given to bringing public understanding in line with operating realities or to finding a more appropriate balance among the impulses that are pressuring the sector and its leaders. In a sense, to survive in a demanding environment, nonprofit organizations are being forced to surrender what may be too many of the things that make them distinctive and worthy of the special advantages they enjoy. Of special note in recent years has been the growing impact of the commercial/managerial impulse, eclipsing the professional emphasis on effectiveness and the voluntaristic emphasis on expressiveness, and potentially undermining as well much of the sector's historic attention to civic activism.

Nonprofit leaders are not without choices in this process, of course. But their choices are highly constrained by the balance of challenges and opportunities they face. Any account of the "future of nonprofit America" in the face of these impulses must therefore be a story in three parts, focusing first on these challenges and opportunities and the extent to which they support or retard these impulses, then examining how the sector's leaders have responded, and finally assessing the consequences of these responses both for individual organizations and subsectors and for nonprofit America as a whole. Only then will it be possible to suggest what alternative options might be worth considering in order to achieve a more appropriate balance among the impulses at play than seems to be emerging. It is to these tasks that we therefore now turn.

4

The Challenges

Writing in 1981, at the end of a decade that witnessed a renaissance of interest in America's nonprofit organizations, Stuart Langton found reason to declare the dawn of a "new voluntarism" in America and to see in the nation's voluntary organizations "a sector of hope in an age of diminishing expectations" and "a corrective force in American society."[1] Nearly three and a half decades later, Langton's "sector of hope" has become, if not quite a sector of despair, at least a sector in danger. Despite the important contributions they make, nonprofit organizations find themselves at present in a time of testing. Once-sacrosanct tax deductions for charitable contributions have been offered up as part of deficit reduction deals; entitlement programs that fueled nonprofit growth for decades are on the chopping block; and new competitors, some of them taking new institutional forms, are challenging not only the nonprofit sector's market share in fields that nonprofits once dominated, but also its claim to distinctiveness as the sector that uniquely mobilizes private initiative for the common good.[2]

To be sure, nonprofits are not alone in facing significant challenges at the present time. But the challenges facing nonprofit organizations are especially daunting since they go to the heart of the sector's operations and raise questions about its very existence. Against the backdrop painted above, it is therefore necessary to look more closely at these challenges before turning, in a subsequent section, to the opportunities the sector also faces. Fundamentally, six such challenges seem especially significant. From all indications, moreover, these challenges seem likely to persist, and in some cases to intensify, in the years ahead.

The Fiscal Challenge

In the first place, America's nonprofit organizations confront a significant fiscal squeeze. This fiscal squeeze has waxed and waned over the sector's recent history stretching from 1965 to the present, but the current period appears to mark a new level of severity. To see this, the discussion here examines the period of government-fueled fiscal growth from 1965 to 1980, the period of retrenchment that followed in the 1980s, the partial recovery that ensued from 1990 to 2007, and the further strains triggered by the 2008 financial crisis.

The Great Society and Beyond, 1965–80

Fiscal distress has been a way of life for the nonprofit sector throughout its history, but this eased significantly during World War II and even more so during the 1960s, when the federal government expanded its funding, first, of scientific research, and then of a wide range of health and social services. Thus, as shown in figure 4-1, government social welfare spending grew at a robust average annual rate of 6.8 percent during the 1965–80 period, driven largely by the 8.2 percent average annual growth in federal social welfare spending as the social programs of President Lyndon Johnson's Great Society kicked in.[3]

Though it is not widely recognized, governmental efforts to stimulate scientific advance and overcome poverty and ill health during this period relied heavily on nonprofit organizations for their operation, following a

Figure 4-1. *Average Annual Change in Government Social Welfare Spending, 1965–2013 (Inflation Adjusted)*

Percent change in government spending

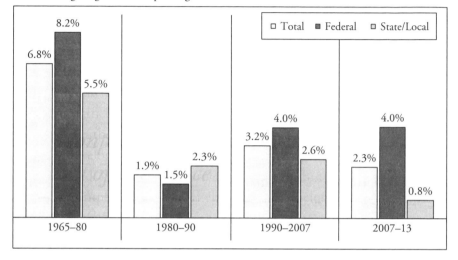

Source: NIPA table 3.16 (2007–11); all other periods from figure 1-5 in Lester M. Salamon, ed., *The State of Nonprofit America*, 2nd ed. (Brookings, 2012). See also chapter 4, note 3.

Note: Includes housing and community services, health, education, and income security, including retirement, unemployment assistance, and social services.

pattern that was established early in this nation's history.[4] By the late 1970s, as a consequence, federal support alone to American nonprofit organizations outdistanced private charitable support by a factor of two to one, while state and local governments provided additional aid.[5] What is more, this support percolated through a wide swath of the sector, providing needed financial nourishment to universities, hospitals, clinics, day care centers, nursing homes, employment and training centers, family service agencies, and many more. Indeed, much of the modern nonprofit sector as we know it took shape during this period as a direct outgrowth of expanded government support.

Federal Retrenchment, 1980–90

This widespread government support to nonprofit organizations suffered a significant shock, however, in the early 1980s. Committed to a policy of fiscal restraint and inspired by the goal of restoring the voluntaristic impulse to the nonprofit sector ("We have let government take away too many of the things that were once ours to do voluntarily," is how Ronald Reagan put it in one of his first speeches as president), the Reagan administration launched a serious assault on federal spending in precisely the areas where federal support to nonprofit organizations was most extensive—social and human services, education and training, community development, and nonhospital health care.

Although the budget cuts that occurred were not as severe as proposed, federal support to nonprofit organizations, outside of Medicare and Medicaid, declined by approximately 25 percent in real dollar terms in the early 1980s and did not return to its 1980 level until the latter 1990s.[6] Some state governments boosted their own spending in many of these fields, but not nearly enough to offset the federal cuts. Indeed, as figure 4-1 shows, total government social welfare spending grew at an anemic average annual rate of 1.9 percent during the 1980–90 decade, well below the growth of the population, and even this was largely due to the growth of the major entitlement programs of Social Security and Medicare, which the Reagan administration chose not to touch. Outside of pensions, public education, and health, however, overall government social welfare spending declined by more than $30 billion between 1981 and 1989. Nonprofit organizations in the fields of community development, employment and training, social services, and community health were particularly hard hit by these reductions.

Partial Resumption of Government Social Welfare
Spending Growth, 1990–2007

Government social welfare spending resumed its growth in the 1990s and into the new century, but at a much slower average rate than during the 1965–80 period. A number of factors seem to have been responsible for this growth:

—*Expansion of entitlement program coverage.* Responding to various constituencies whose needs remained inadequately addressed by the social programs of the Great Society, especially in the wake of the

Reagan retrenchment of the 1980s and the Contract for America cuts introduced in the mid-1990s, Congress expanded eligibility under the basic government entitlement programs for health and income assistance. For example, coverage under the federal Supplemental Security Income program, which was originally created to provide income support to the elderly poor, was expanded to cover people with disabilities, including children and youth, increasing the number of recipients by 50 percent, from 4.1 million in 1980 to 6.6 million by 1999.[7] And similar extensions of coverage occurred in Medicaid and other entitlement programs.[8]

—*New federal initiatives.* In addition to expanding coverage under existing programs, federal policymakers also created programs to address long-standing or newly emerging social ills. For example, four federal child care programs were added in 1988 and 1990 alone, and special programs were added as well for homeless people, AIDS sufferers, children and youth, people with disabilities, voluntarism promotion, drug and alcohol treatment, and home health care.[9]

—*Medicalization of aid.* In the face of cuts to discretionary grant programs, many states found ways to shift activities previously funded from state resources or federal discretionary programs subjected to Reagan-era budget cuts, and reconfigure them to make them eligible for funding under the more lucrative Medicaid or SSI entitlement programs.[10]

—*The welfare reform windfall.* Passage in 1996 of the Personal Responsibility and Work Opportunity Reconciliation Act (welfare reform) produced its own windfall of resources in program areas of interest to nonprofits. This was so because the act replaced the existing program of entitlement grants for welfare recipients channeled through states with fixed, six-year federal grants to states for use in both direct payments to welfare recipients and, if funds were available, programs supporting work readiness, child care, and human services to help welfare recipients transition into work. When welfare rolls began to fall sharply in the late 1990s thanks to the

economic boom then in progress, the funds needed for direct payments to beneficiaries declined, and states found themselves with
a fiscal windfall that they were able to invest in expanded service
programs designed to prepare even more welfare recipients for work.
As a result, the social welfare system was temporarily awash with
funds.[11]

Although government support of the nonprofit sector resumed its
growth in the 1990s and into the new millennium, albeit at a slower pace,
the experience of the 1980s and early 1990s left behind a lingering
residue of anxiety that has still not subsided. This anxiety was reignited,
moreover, by the conservative revolt that produced the Contract with
America experience of the mid-1990s, with its calls for further sharp reductions in government social welfare spending, and by the additional
significant cuts in discretionary programs of interest to nonprofits proposed by the Bush administration beginning in 2002.[12]

Return of Retrenchment, 2008 Onward

More recently, the banking crisis and resulting recession that began in
2008 added new causes for concern. To be sure, the economic recovery
program passed by Congress in early 2009 helped to buffer many human
service nonprofits from the early effects of this recession, and the operation of the nation's still largely intact social safety net provided at least
partial relief to the growing numbers of the nation's unemployed. As a
consequence, overall government social welfare spending rose at an annual rate of 2.3 percent between 2007 and 2013, much of it buoyed by
spending on federal health, food, unemployment, and related entitlement
programs. But a shift in the country's political climate, following the rise
of the Tea Party movement and the passage of the Obama administration's health reform plan, all but slammed the door on additional antire-
cessionary assistance or expanded government support for social welfare
assistance, while concern about the substantial federal deficit bequeathed
by the Bush-era tax cuts and costly wars in Iraq and Afghanistan made
it increasingly clear that the government's past role as a major source of

nonprofit revenue growth was likely to be scaled back extensively. With powerful political forces insisting that deficit reduction proceed entirely, or at least chiefly, through spending cuts as opposed to revenue increases, the stage was set for another extended period, if not of actual retrenchment, then at least of limited new growth.[13] As we will see, moreover, this came on top of actual declines in charitable support as well. What is more, stressed by the recession, state and local spending on social welfare could not manage even 1 percent of real growth.

From Producer Subsidies to Consumer Subsidies

Furthermore, not just the amount, but also the form, of public sector support to the nonprofit sector changed during this period. Where in the 1960s and 1970s the federal government offered grants and contracts to nonprofit organizations and gave nonprofits the inside track, the ascendance of conservative political elements in the 1980s and beyond brought with it a conscious effort through executive office circulars and other vehicles to encourage government program managers to promote *for-profit* involvement in government contract work instead, including that for human services.[14] At the same time, given the prevailing climate of tax cuts and hostility to expanded government spending throughout the 1980s and into the 1990s, policymakers increasingly responded to social welfare and related needs by relying more heavily on less conventional tools of government action, such as loan guarantees, tax expenditures, and vouchers, which channel aid to the consumers of services instead of the producers, thus requiring nonprofits to compete for clients in the market, where for-profits have traditionally had the edge.[15]

The use of such tools is by no means entirely new, of course. The deduction for medical expenses and the exclusion of scholarship income, for example, have long been established features of the tax code. But the use of such tools in fields where nonprofits are active expanded considerably during the 1990s and into the new century, with the addition or extension of programs such as the child care tax credit, the credit for student loan interest payments, the low-income housing tax credit, and the new market tax credit. Just three of these tools—tax expenditures, loan guarantees, and direct loans—amounted as of 2010 to $484.1 billion in federal assistance in fields where nonprofits are active. This is nearly double their scale two decades earlier, even after adjusting for inflation, as shown in table 4-1, and roughly equivalent to the more than $500 billion in total direct government support flowing to nonprofits. In many fields, the indirect subsidies available through the tax system easily exceed those supported by the outright spending programs. In day care, for example, the $4.4 billion in subsidies made available to middle-income and lower-middle-income families through the child and dependent care tax credit in 2014 was nearly twice as large as the roughly $2.3 billion in subsidies provided to poor families through the Child Care and Development Block Grant.[16] And these figures do not even include the massive sums spent through the two sizable federal voucher programs, Medicare and Medicaid. Already by 1980, as a consequence, the majority (53 percent) of federal assistance to nonprofit organizations took the form of such consumer-side subsidies, much of it through the Medicare and Medicaid programs. By 1986 this stood at 70 percent, and it continued to rise into the 1990s and beyond.

In part, this shift toward consumer-side subsidies resulted from the concentration of budget cuts almost exclusively on the so-called discretionary spending programs, which tend to be producer-side grant and contract programs, while Medicare and Medicaid—both of them demand-side subsidies—continued to grow.[17] In part also, however, the shift toward

Table 4-1. *Growth in Federal Tax Expenditure and Loan Programs Relevant to Nonprofit Organizations, 1990–2010, in Constant 2010 Dollars*

	Amount ($billions)		
Tool	*1990*	*2010*	*% change, 1990–2010*
Tax expenditures	201.2	292.5	45.4%
Direct loans	0.2	149.4	84,846.2%
Loan guarantees	47.3	42.3	−10.6%
TOTAL	248.7	484.1	94.7%

Source: U.S. Office of Management and Budget, Budget of the U.S. Government, FY2012, Supplemental Tables; U.S. Office of Management and Budget, Budget of the U.S. Government, FY1992, Special Analyses.

consumer-side subsidies reflects the ascendance of conservative political forces that favor forms of assistance that maximize consumer choice. The price of securing conservative support for new or expanded programs of relevance to nonprofit organizations in the latter 1980s and 1990s, therefore, was to structure them as vouchers or tax expenditures, and that sentiment survived into the 2000s. The new Child Care and Development Block Grant enacted in 1990, and then reauthorized and expanded as part of the welfare reform legislation in 1996, thus specifically gave states the option to use the $5 billion in federal funds provided for day care to finance voucher payments to eligible families rather than grants or contracts to day care providers, and most states have pursued this option. As of 1998, therefore, well over 80 percent of the children receiving day care assistance under this program were receiving it through such voucher certificates, and another $4.4 billion in federal day care subsidies is delivered through a special child care tax credit.[18] Compared to this $7 billion in consumer-side subsidies for day care, the total that the federal government makes available through its producer-side social services block grant for the full range of social services, including day care, stood at only $2.8 billion.

Nonprofit day care providers, like their counterparts in other fields, have thus been thrown increasingly into the private market to secure even public funding for their activities. As a result, they have been obliged to master complex billing and reimbursement systems and to learn how to "market" their services to potential "customers." Worse yet, the reimbursement rates in many of these programs have often failed to keep pace with rising costs, putting a further squeeze on nonprofit budgets and making it harder to sustain mission-critical functions such as advocacy and charity care.

Not only did government support to nonprofit organizations change its form during this period, but so did important elements of private support. The most notable development here was the emergence of "managed care" in the health field, displacing the traditional pattern of fee-for-service medicine. Medicare provided an important impetus for this development by replacing its cost-based reimbursement system for hospitals in the early 1980s with a system of fixed payments for particular procedures.

Corporations, too, responded to the rapid escalation of health care benefits for their workers by moving aggressively during the 1990s to replace
standard fee-for-service insurance plans with managed care plans that
featured up-front capitation payments to managed care providers. These
providers then inserted themselves between patients and health care providers, negotiating rates with the providers and deciding which procedures were truly necessary. By 1997, close to 75 percent of the employees
in medium and large establishments, and 62 percent of the employees in
small establishments, were covered by some type of managed care plan.[19]
More recently, managed care has expanded into the social services field,
subjecting nonprofit drug treatment, rehabilitation service, and mental
health treatment facilities to the same competitive pressures and reimbursement limits as hospitals have been confronting.

Taken together, these shifts added significant force to the commercialism impulse pressing on the nonprofit sector. The new forms of public
action put a premium on skills and capacities far different from those
advantaged by the other impulses outlined in the previous chapter. To
survive in this new government marketplace, nonprofits had to adapt to
the new commercial realities, find new market niches, or surrender market share. As we will see, most did some of each.[20]

Tepid Growth in Philanthropic Support

Adding to the fiscal pressure nonprofits face has been the inability of private philanthropy to offset cutbacks in government support and finance
expanded nonprofit responses to community needs. To be sure, private
giving has grown considerably in the recent past. Between 1977 and 1997,
for example, total private giving grew by some 90 percent after adjusting
for inflation, roughly equivalent to the growth of gross domestic product. However, this lumps the amounts provided for the actual operations
of charities in a given year with large endowment gifts to foundations,
universities, and other institutions—gifts typically not available for use
in a given year—as well as with gifts to religious congregations, most of
which go to the upkeep of the congregations and clergy.[21] When we focus
on the private gifts available to support nonprofit human service, arts,

education, health, and advocacy organizations over this twenty-year period, the growth rate was closer to 62 percent—still impressive, but well below the 96 percent growth in overall nonprofit revenue.[22] Indeed, as a share of personal income, private giving declined steadily in the United States between the 1970s and the early 1990s, from an average of 1.86 percent in the 1970s, to 1.78 percent in the 1980s, and to 1.72 percent in the early 1990s. As a share of total sector income, private giving outside of giving to religion thus actually lost ground between 1977 and 1997, falling from 18 percent of the total in 1977 to 10 percent in 1997. With giving to religion included, the total declined from 26 percent to 17.5 percent.[23]

Giving grew somewhat more robustly in the more recent 1997–2007 period, but the amounts reaching nonprofit service and expressive organizations did not come close to returning the giving share of total organization income to the levels that existed in the late 1970s. Thus, as shown in table 4-2, outside of religion, giving to nonprofit service and expressive organizations registered a sizable 64 percent growth during this decade, compared to a growth of 53 percent in the overall revenue of these organizations. However, because it started from such a small base, giving barely held its own as a share of total revenue for these organizations, increasing from 9.5 percent of the total in 1997 to 10.0 percent in 2007. And with the onset of the 2008 recession and the shrinking of assets caused by the housing bust and the banking crisis, the growth rate of private giving not only slowed, but actually reversed, ending up, as of 2011, still 2 percent below its 2007 level in inflation-adjusted terms, and

Table 4-2. *Shifts in Private Giving and Total Nonprofit Revenue, 1997–2007, in Constant Dollars*

Type of recipient organization	% change, 1997–2007		Giving as % of total revenue	
	Private giving	*Total revenue*	*1997*	*2007*
Service and expressive	+64%	+53%	9.5%	10.0%
Religious congregations	+21%	+25%	88.0%	85.0%
All	+42%	+50%	17.5%	16.6%

Source: Internal Revenue Service Statistics of Income Microdata Files. See chapter 4, note 23.

declining from 10.0 percent of nonprofit service and expressive organization revenue in 2007 to 9.4 percent in 2011.[74]

The Competition Challenge

In addition to a fiscal challenge, nonprofit America has also faced a serious competitive challenge as a result of a significant growth of for-profit involvement in many traditional fields of nonprofit activity, from health care and welfare assistance to higher education and employment training. This, too, is not a wholly new development. Thus the nonprofit share of day care jobs dropped from 52 percent to 38 percent between 1982 and 1997, a 27 percent loss of market share. Similarly sharp declines in the relative nonprofit share occurred among rehabilitation hospitals (down 50 percent), home health agencies (down 48 percent), health maintenance organizations (down 60 percent), kidney dialysis centers (down 45 percent), hospices (down 15 percent), and mental health clinics (down 11 percent). In many of these fields the absolute number of nonprofit facilities continued to grow, but the for-profit growth outpaced it. And in at least one crucial field—acute care hospitals—while the nonprofit share increased slightly, a significant reduction occurred in the *absolute number* of nonprofit (as well as public) facilities, so that the for-profit share of the total increased even more.[25]

That these reductions have continued and spread into broader fields in more recent years is evident in table 4-3. Thus, between 1997 and 2012, relative to for-profit employment, the nonprofit share of kidney dialysis center employment declined another 41 percent, of home health employment by 33 percent, and of community care for the elderly facility employment by 23 percent. Even classical fields of nonprofit activity such as individual and family services, in which nonprofits had managed to hold their own, have lost ground to for-profit providers in recent years. With over 90 percent of all private individual and family service employment as recently as 1997, nonprofits found themselves with just over 60 percent fifteen years later, in 2012, a 30 percent drop in market share.[26]

Table 4-3.   *Change in Nonprofit Share of Employment, Selected Fields,*
1997–2012

NAICS code	Type of organization	% change, 1997–2012
621492	Kidney dialysis centers	−41%
621610	Home health care services	−33%
6241	Individual and family services	−30%
6233	Community care facilities for the elderly	−23%
6223	Specialty hospitals (except psychiatric)	−20%
6214	Outpatient care centers	−13%
6231	Nursing care facilities	−11%
6239	Other residential care facilities	−6%
6244	Child day care services	−3%

Source: U.S. Bureau of the Census, *Economic Census, 1997, 2012.*

The range of for-profit firms competing with nonprofits has broadened, moreover. For example, the recent welfare reform legislation, which seeks to move large numbers of welfare recipients from welfare dependence to employment, attracted defense contractors like Lockheed Martin to the social welfare field. What these firms offer is less knowledge of human services than information-processing technology and contract management skills gained from serving as master contractors on huge military system projects, precisely the skills now needed to manage the subcontracting systems required to prepare welfare recipients for work.[27] Similarly, for-profits have made substantial inroads in the field of higher education. Between 1980 and 2005, while enrollment in public and nonprofit higher education institutions each grew by roughly 37 percent, enrollment in for-profit institutions expanded by 800 percent—from just over 110,000 to more than 1 million students.[28] Even the field of charitable fundraising has recently experienced a further significant for-profit incursion in the form of financial service firms such as Fidelity and Schwab, which have created their own closely associated charitable gift funds. By 2000 the Fidelity Charitable Gift Fund had attracted more assets than the nation's largest community foundation and distributed three times as much in grants.[29] Taken together, as of 2007 the assets held in the donor-advised funds managed by the thirty-eight corporate-originated charitable funds exceeded the donor-advised-fund holdings of all six hundred of the nation's community foundations.[30]

The reasons for this striking for-profit success are by no means clear and vary from field to field. The shift in forms of public funding mentioned earlier has very likely played a significant role: by shifting from producer-side subsidies to consumer-side subsidies, the federal government channeled more of its assistance through the marketplace, where for-profit firms have a natural advantage. The rise of managed care and other "third-party payment" methods discussed earlier in this chapter have had a similar effect, since such arrangements put a special premium on price rather than quality or community roots in choosing providers, thus minimizing the comparative advantages of nonprofits.

Perhaps most decisive in explaining why nonprofits have lost market share to for-profits in so many markets, however, is the uneven playing field nonprofits confront in accessing the investment capital required to establish new facilities and new operations in response to technological changes or rapid surges in demand such as often occur when new government programs are created. A recent survey by the Johns Hopkins Nonprofit Listening Post Project found, for example, that the overwhelming majority of nonprofit organizations in the core human service, arts, and community development fields need investment capital to acquire facilities, equipment, and strategic planning.[31] Because they are prohibited from distributing profits to their "owners" (and indeed are not allowed to have "owners" in the market sense of the word), nonprofits lack access to the essentially "free" capital that for-profit businesses can generate merely by issuing and selling stock. Most of these surveyed organizations therefore encountered difficulties accessing the investment capital they needed, and those that did manage to access it were restricted to borrowing from commercial banks, typically the most expensive sources.

When surges in demand occur, such as accompanied the decision in 1980 to make home health care a reimbursable expense under the federal government's Medicare Program as a way to reduce the spiraling cost of hospital care, it is for-profit providers who are in the best position to respond, in this case by floating IPOs (initial public offerings) and generating the capital to build thousands of new facilities. And this pattern has been repeated in numerous other spheres. While efforts have recently been launched to attract private investment capital to "social enterprises" and other social-purpose organizations, and to entice foundations to function like "philanthropic banks" by leveraging their assets to incentivize such flows of private investment capital into nonprofit and for-profit social ventures, such efforts remain on the "frontiers" of philanthropic and private-investment practice and have yet to be fully mainstreamed.[32]

The Effectiveness Challenge

One consequence of the increased competition nonprofits are facing has been to intensify the pressure on them to perform—and to demonstrate that performance. The result is a third challenge: the effectiveness challenge. As the management expert William Ryan writes, "Nonprofits are now forced to reexamine their reasons for existing in light of a market that rewards discipline and performance and emphasizes organizational capacity rather than for-profit or nonprofit status and mission. Nonprofits have no choice but to reckon with these forces."[33] This runs counter to long-standing theories in the nonprofit field that emphasize this sector's distinctive advantage precisely in fields where normal market mechanisms do not operate because the consumers of services are not the same as the people paying for them, and where trust is consequently needed instead. Because they are not organized to pursue profits, it is argued, nonprofits are more worthy of such trust and therefore more reliable providers in such difficult-to-measure fields.[34]

In the current climate, however, such theories have few remaining adherents, at least among those who control the sector's purse strings. Government managers, themselves under pressure to demonstrate results as a consequence of the recent Government Performance and Results Act, are increasingly pressing their nonprofit contractors to deliver measurable results, too. Not to be outdone, prominent philanthropic institutions have jumped onto the performance bandwagon. United Way of America, for example, thus launched a bold performance measurement system in the mid-1990s, complete with website, performance measurement manual, and video, in order to induce member agencies to require performance measurement as a condition of local funding. Numerous foundations have moved in a similar direction, increasing the emphasis on evaluation both of their grantees and of their own programming.[35] Indeed, a new foundation affinity group, Grantmakers for Effective Organizations (GEO), was recently formed, and a new "venture philanthropy" model has been attracting adherents.[36] The key to this model is an investment approach to grantmaking that calls on philanthropic institutions to invest in organizations rather than individual programs, to take a more active hand in organizational governance and operations, and to insist on measurable results. This same emphasis on "metrics" as the new elixir of nonprofit performance has taken root in the social enterprise movement that has lately swept the nonprofit field, with support from a new class of dot.com entrepreneurs turned philanthropists.[37]

The resulting "accountability environment" in which nonprofits are having to operate will doubtless produce many positive results. But it also increases the pressures on hard-pressed nonprofit managers for demonstrations of progress that neither they, nor anyone else, may be able to supply, at least not without far greater resources than are currently available for the task. What is more, accountability expectations often fail to acknowledge the multiple meanings that accountability can have and the multiple stakeholders whose accountability demands nonprofits must accommodate.[38] The risk is great, therefore, that the measures most readily at hand, or those most responsive to the market test, will substitute for those most germane to the problems being addressed. That, at any rate, is the lesson of public sector experience with performance measurement, and the increased focus on price rather than quality or community benefit in third-party contracting with nonprofit health providers certainly supports this observation.[39]

The Technology Challenge

Pressures from for-profit competitors have also accelerated the demands on nonprofits to incorporate new technology into their operations. Indeed, technology has become one of the wild cards of nonprofit evolution.

But enticing as the opportunities opened by technological change may be to the nation's nonprofit institutions, they pose at least equally enormous challenges. Most obvious, perhaps, are the financial challenges. As one recent study has noted, "Information technologies are resource intensive. They entail significant purchase costs, require significant training and upkeep, and yet become obsolete quickly."[40] Because of the structural disadvantages nonprofits face in raising capital due to their inability to enter the equity markets, however, the massive intrusion of new technological requirements into their work puts them at a distinct disadvantage vis-à-vis their for-profit competitors. We have already seen the consequences of this in the health insurance industry, where the lack of capital following the discontinuation of government funding led to loss of market share to for-profit firms, which were better able to capitalize the huge investments in information-processing equipment required to manage the large risk pools that make managed care viable. Similar pressures are now at work in the social services industry, where managed care is also taking root.

Not only does technology threaten to alter further the balance between nonprofits and for-profits, but it also threatens to alter the structure of the nonprofit sector itself, advantaging larger organizations over smaller ones. This is due in part to the heavy fixed costs of the new technology. Already, concerns about a "digital divide" are surfacing within the sector, as survey after survey reveals the unequal distribution of both hardware and the capacity to adapt the hardware to organizational missions.[41] Though it initially stimulates competition by giving even small start-ups access to huge markets, information technology also creates "network effects" that accentuate the advantages of dominant players.[42] Concern has thus surfaced that e-philanthropy will allow large, well-known national nonprofits to raid the donor bases of local United Ways and operating charities and that information technology more generally advantages large, nationally prominent agencies in the competition for business partners, government funding, and charitable support. Although recent data suggest that more nonprofits are managing to catch up to the early adopters with respect to core IT tools, such as computers and Internet access, many fewer nonprofits are using newer technologies, such as hand-held devices and web applications. What is more, technology is being applied more extensively to basic administrative and accounting functions than to more complex programmatic ones.[43]

But the challenges posed by technology go far beyond financial or competitive considerations. Also at stake are fundamental philosophical issues that go to the heart of the nonprofit sector's mission and modes of operation. Indeed, technology has been one of the doors through which the commercial impulse has entered the nonprofit sector in a major way. Such issues have surfaced especially vividly in the arts, where the new technology raises fundamental questions of aesthetics, creative control, and intellectual property rights.[44] Similar dilemmas confront educational institutions that are tempted by the new technologies to brand their products and package them for mass consumption, but at the risk of alienating their professorate, losing the immediacy of direct student-faculty contact, and giving precedence to the packaging of knowledge rather than to its discovery. How these commercial/technological dilemmas are resolved could well determine how the nonprofit sector evolves in the years ahead.

The Legitimacy Challenge

The moral and philosophical challenges that American nonprofit organizations are confronting at the present time go well beyond those posed by new technology, however. Rather, a serious fault line seems to have opened in the foundation of public trust on which the entire nonprofit edifice rests. This may be due in part to the unrealistic expectations that the public has of these institutions, expectations that the charitable sector ironically counts on and encourages. Also at work, however, have been four other lines of argument.

The Special Interest Argument

The first is the strident indictment that conservative politicians and commentators have lodged against many nonprofit organizations over the past decade or more, on grounds that nonprofit charitable organizations have become just another special interest, regularly conspiring with government bureaucrats to escalate public spending, and doing so less out of real conviction about the needs being served than a desire to feather their own nests. The Heritage Foundation president Edward Feulner put this case especially sharply in 1996, criticizing charities for urging Congress to expand social welfare spending while themselves "feeding at the public trough."[45] Entire organizations have been formed, in fact, to remove the halo from the nonprofit sector in this way, charging that a "new kind of nonprofit organization" has emerged in recent years "dedicated not to voluntary action, but to an expanded government role in our lives."[46]

Worse than that, the very motives of nonprofit agencies have been called into question. Involvement in government programs "changes charities' incentives," charges one critique, "giving them reasons to keep caseloads up instead of getting them down by successfully turning around people's lives."[47] Nonprofits thus stand accused not only of being ineffective but also of preferring not to solve the problems they are purportedly addressing. In part to remedy this, advocates of this view rallied behind the so-called Istook amendment, which sought to limit the advocacy activity of nonprofit organizations by prohibiting any nonprofit organization receiving government support from using more than 5 percent of its *total* revenues, not just its government revenues, for advocacy or lobbying activities.

The Programmatic Critique

Feeding into this critique, moreover, has been a second line of argument that has caught nonprofit organizations, particularly in the human service field, in the more general assault on public social programs that has animated national political debate for more than three decades now. In the minds of many, the persistence of poverty, urban crime, teenage pregnancy, and numerous other problems has been taken as evidence that publicly funded social programs do not work, despite considerable evidence to the contrary.[48] The resulting open season on government social programs has caught significant components of the nonprofit sector in the crossfire, particularly since the sector has been involved in administering many of the discredited efforts. Underlying this argument is a profound rethinking of the causes of poverty and of the interventions likely to reduce it. The central change here involves a loss of faith in the traditional premise of professional social work, with its emphasis on casework and individualized services as the cure for poverty and disadvantage. During the 1960s, this precept was translated into public policy through the 1962 amendments to the Social Security Act and, later, through portions of the Economic Opportunity Act of 1964, both of which made federal resources available to purchase social services for poor people in the hope that this would allow them to escape the "culture of poverty" in which they were enmeshed. In the process, the professionalism impulse was firmly implanted in the nation's nonprofit sector.

This "services strategy," and the professionalism impulse it encouraged, has subsequently been challenged by critics on both the right and the left. Those on the right argue that the growth of supportive services and income assistance for the poor ultimately creates disincentives to work and undermines fundamental values of self-reliance.[49] Those on the left, by contrast, point to the structural shifts in the economy, which have eliminated much of the market for blue-collar labor, as the real causes of poverty, unemployment, and the social maladies that flow from them. Both sides seem to agree, however, that the traditional skills of the nonprofit human service sector have become increasingly irrelevant to the problems facing the poor. More important than social services in the new paradigm is job readiness and, ultimately, a job.

Under these circumstances, the employer rather than the social worker becomes the pivot of social policy. While private nonprofit organizations may still play a role in the alleviation of poverty, the real action has shifted to the business community, the educational system, and, in the conservative view, the faith community. This is clearly reflected in the welfare reform law of 1996, which ended the entitlement to income assistance and emphasized employment as a condition of assistance.

These views also echoed loudly in the Bush administration's 2001 proposal to privilege "faith-based charities" in the distribution of federal assistance. A principal appeal of this idea is the prospect of replacing formal, professionalized nonprofit organizations with informal church groups, staffed by well-meaning volunteers, who can help individuals gain the life skills and moral backbone thought to be needed to succeed in the workplace. This is consistent with the "voluntarism" impulse and reinforces a quaint, nineteenth-century image of how charitable organizations are supposed to operate, an image that competitive pressures, accountability demands, and technological change have made increasingly untenable. This jobs focus also lies behind the recent enthusiasm for "social enterprises," which, unlike standard human service agencies, use the market to pursue social objectives.[50] All of this has pushed the traditional nonprofit sector toward the periphery of social problem solving, at least in much of the prevailing political rhetoric, undermining the professional impulse and strengthening the civic activism, voluntaristic, and commercial impulses at work in the sector.

The Overprofessionalization Argument

Similar challenges to the legitimacy of nonprofit organizations and to the professional impulse that gained ascendance in much of the nonprofit sector over the previous half century arise from critics who take nonprofits to task for becoming overly professional and thus losing touch with those they serve. This line of argument has a long lineage in American social science, as evidenced by the brilliant analysis by the historian Roy Lubove of the professionalization of social work, which led social workers away from social diagnosis, community organizing, and social reform toward a client-focused, medical model of social work practice.[51]

More recently, critics on the left have implicated nonprofit organizations more generally for contributing to the overprofessionalization of social concerns, redefining basic human needs as "problems" that only professionals can resolve, and thereby alienating people from the helping relationships they could establish with their neighbors and kin.[52] By embracing professionalism, these critics charge, nonprofit organizations destroy community rather than building it. Critics on the right, moreover, have been equally derisive of the professionalized human service apparatus, charging it with inflating the cost of dealing with social problems by "crowding" out lower-cost, alternative mechanisms that are at least as effective.[53] This, in turn, has added further fuel to the voluntarism engine.

The Accountability Argument

Complicating matters further is the fact that nonprofit organizations generally lack meaningful bases for demonstrating the value of what they do. "Unlike publicly traded companies," the management expert Regina Herzlinger notes, "the performance of nonprofits and governments is shrouded behind a veil of secrecy that is lifted only when blatant disasters occur."[54] This is problematic, she argues, because nonprofit organizations generally lack the three basic accountability mechanisms of business: the self-interest of owners, competition, and the ultimate bottom-line measure of profitability. This view has prompted calls even from advocates of the sector for more formal mechanisms for holding nonprofit organizations accountable and suggestions from political leaders that the nonprofit sector is in serious need of additional regulation.[55]

Consequences

These criticisms, coupled with a spate of high-profile scandals in the early 1990s, seem to have shaken public confidence in charitable institutions. Surveys taken in 1994 and 1996 found only 33 percent and 37 percent of respondents, respectively, expressing "a great deal" or "quite a lot" of confidence in nonprofit human service agencies, well behind the proportions expressing similar levels of confidence in the military and small business.[56] This improved considerably in the latter 1990s, perhaps as a consequence of the perceived success of welfare reform. Yet even at this latter date, while a substantial majority of respondents agreed that "charitable organizations play a major role in making our communities better places to live," only 20 percent "strongly agreed" with this statement. And only 10 percent agreed "strongly" that most charities are "honest and ethical in their use of donated funds," a figure that remained at this low level in 2006, seven years later.[57] All of this suggests that America's nonprofit institutions are delicately balanced on a knife edge of public support, with most people willing to grant them the benefit of the doubt, but with a strong undercurrent of uncertainty and concern. As a consequence, a relative handful of highly visible scandals—such as the United Way scandal of the early 1990s, the New Era Philanthropy scandal of the mid-1990s, or the Red Cross difficulties in the wake of September 11— can have an impact that goes well beyond their actual significance.

Taking advantage of the resulting questioning, local governments are increasingly emboldened to challenge the tax exemptions of nonprofit organizations. Such challenges have surfaced in Pennsylvania, New York, New Hampshire, Oregon, Maine, Wisconsin, Colorado, Massachusetts, and Illinois.[58] A recent survey showed, in fact, that among one sample of mostly midsize and large nonprofits operating in the fields of social services, community development, and arts and culture, a striking 63 percent reported currently paying some kind of tax, payment in lieu of taxes, or other fee to state or local government.[59] And challenges to the favorable tax treatment of nonprofits are not restricted to state and local governments. As noted earlier, the Obama administration, hardly a foe of the nonprofit sector, proposed a cap on the tax deduction available for charitable contributions in its 2012 budget proposal and repeated this idea in the deficit reduction proposals it advanced during the debt crisis debate of 2011.

One additional reflection of the legitimacy cloud under which nonprofits have been obliged to operate concerns their political advocacy activities, another crucial function of the nonprofit sector, as outlined in chapter 2. To be sure, restrictions on nonprofit campaign activities and lobbying have long been a part of the basic federal tax exemption law. But *lobbying* is defined rather narrowly in the tax law, and even then nonprofits are allowed to engage in it as long as it does not constitute a "significant" part of their activities. Beginning in the late 1960s, and then gathering pace in the 1980s and over the next twenty-five years, however, nonprofits have been subjected to an increasing set of restrictions on their advocacy and lobbying activities. These restrictions are all the more troubling for nonprofits in view of the 2010 Supreme Court ruling in *Citizens United* v. *Federal Election Commission,* which removed all restrictions on corporate financing of election campaigns.[60] An opening salvo in this line of restrictions came with the passage of the landmark 1969 Tax Act, which penalized foundations for their involvement in the civil rights struggle of the 1960s by prohibiting foundations from financing nonprofit efforts to influence legislation, thus eliminating one of the more important sources of funding for nonprofit lobbying activities.[61] This was followed by an Office of Management and Budget Circular (A-122) promulgated by the Reagan administration in 1984, which essentially prohibits nonprofits from using federal grant dollars to support "political advocacy," a concept that embraces far more than the narrow concept of "lobbying."[62] The Lobbying Disclosure Act of 1995 then extended restrictions on lobbying to 501(c)(4) organizations, which are specifically permitted to lobby even if they receive federal grants, loans, or awards. A spate of general campaign finance and lobby disclosure restrictions in 2002, 2004, and 2007 also caught nonprofit organizations in the crossfire.[63] And nonprofits have also confronted additional challenges, so far unsuccessful, to bar organizations receiving federal funds not only from attempting to influence legislation but also from engaging in litigation or participating in administrative agency proceedings, activities long considered fundamental forms of expression in a free society.

The Human Resource Challenge

Inevitably, fiscal stress and signs of public ambivalence toward the nonprofit sector have taken their toll on the sector's human resources. Experts in the child welfare field, for example, identify "staff turnover" as "perhaps the most important problem" facing the field, and cite "stress, . . . overwhelming accountability requirements, and concern over liability" as the principal causes.[64] Similar problems afflict the international relief field due to the explosion of complex humanitarian crises that intermix enormous relief challenges with complicated political and military conflicts.[65] More generally, a recent survey of close to 2,000 nonprofit organizations by HR Report found that attracting and retaining qualified talent is "one of the greatest challenges facing nonprofits."[66]

Especially difficult has been the recruitment and retention of front-line service workers, for whom salary, benefit, and safety issues are particularly important, but retention of managerial personnel has also grown increasingly problematic. One study of graduates of public policy programs reports, for example, that the proportion of these public-spirited young people who took their first jobs in nonprofit organizations doubled between the early 1970s and the early 1990s.[67] However, the nonprofit sector's retention rate for these personnel has declined over time, with more turning to the for-profit sector as an alternative. Of special concern is the turnover of talent at the executive director level. Executive directors, who came into the field to pursue the social missions of their agencies, find themselves expected to function instead as aggressive entrepreneurs, leading outward-oriented enterprises able to attract paying customers while retaining the allegiance of socially committed donors and boards, all of this in a context of growing public scrutiny and mistrust. According to one study, a surprising two-thirds of the executive directors in a national sample of nonprofit agencies were in their first executive director position, and over half of these had held the job for four years or less.[68] While most reported enjoying their jobs, a third indicated an intention to leave it within two years; and even among those likely to take another job in the nonprofit sector, only half indicated that their next job was likely to be as an executive director. As Stefan Toepler and Margaret Wyszomirski report, leadership recruitment has become a particular challenge in the arts field, where the vacancy rate for art museum directors hit a fifteen-year high in 1999, and continues to trouble the field.[69]

Summary

In short, nonprofit America has confronted a difficult set of challenges over the recent past, and many of these challenges seem likely to persist. Fiscal stress, increased competition, rapidly changing technology, and new accountability expectations have significantly expanded the pressures under which these organizations must work, and this has affected the public support these organizations enjoy and their ability to attract and hold staff.

But challenges are not all that nonprofit America has confronted in the recent past. It has also had the benefit of a number of crucial opportunities, many of which seem likely to persist. It is to these opportunities that we therefore now turn.

5

The Opportunities

Side by side with the significant challenges it has faced over the recent past, nonprofit America has also confronted an attractive range of opportunities. To be sure, the presence of opportunities is no guarantee that they will be seized. What is more, opportunities can bring their own risks. Yet no account of nonprofit America can be complete without examining the opportunities that these organizations have enjoyed. Four of these in particular deserve special attention.

Increased Demand for Their Services

In the first place, nonprofit organizations are being affected by a number of demographic trends that are boosting the demand for the kinds of services these organizations provide. Among the more salient of these trends are the following:

—*Aging of the population.* The country's population of seniors seventy-five years and older doubled between 1980 and 2008, on top of a doubling of the sixty-five and older population between 1960 and 2000. This trend seems likely to continue, moreover, with the prospect that the over-seventy-five population will grow by 77 percent between 2010 and 2030, while the overall population of the country will grow by only 20 percent.[1] This will continue boosting the need for nursing home care, assisted living, and other elderly services, fields in which nonprofits have a considerable, if no longer dominant, presence. At the same time, the lengthened life span of the average American is changing the normal education-work-retirement trajectory to something closer to an education-work-contribute trajectory, as baby boomers show up at the doors of nonprofit organizations as volunteers eager to put their skills at the service of others through so-called *encore careers.*[2]

—*Expansion of the labor force participation rate of women.* The labor force participation rate for women jumped from less than 20 percent in 1960 to over 60 percent in 1998 and has been holding at that level ever since. Even more dramatically, the labor force participation rate for married women with children under the age of six rose from 18.6 percent in 1960 to 62 percent in 2009, and for single women with children under six it reached nearly 68 percent.[3] While it is far from clear what impact the job losses that accompanied the recession that began in 2008 will have on this pattern, it seems likely that the increased demand for child care and other household-related services, another significant arena of nonprofit activity, will persist.

—*Shifts in family structure.* Significant changes that have occurred in the American family structure also have important implications for nonprofit agencies. In 1960 there was one divorce for every four marriages. By 1980 this figure had jumped to one divorce for every two marriages, and it has remained there into the new millennium. During this same period, the number of children involved in divorces increased from 463,000 in 1960 to more than 1 million throughout the 1980s and 1990s. Since divorce typically involves a certain amount of emotional trauma and often brings with it significant loss of economic status, this shift also translates into increased need for human services of the sort that many nonprofit agencies offer. Also contributing to this increased demand is the tremendous surge in out-of-wedlock births. Between 1960 and 1980 the proportion of all births that were to unwed mothers increased from 5 percent to 18 percent, and by 1994 it had reached 33 percent. This represents an eightfold increase in the number of out-of-wedlock births, from 224,000 in 1960 to 1.3 million in 1995, and to 1.7 million in 2007. Although this phenomenon is sometimes perceived to be concentrated in minority populations, in fact the vast majority of these births (68 percent) are to white mothers.[4]

—*Substance abuse.* Changes have also occurred in the prevalence of substance abuse in American society. One reflection of this is the striking increase in the number of people receiving substance abuse treatment over the past several decades. As recently as 1977 the number of people using such services stood at approximately 235,000. By 1995 it was over 1 million, and by 2009 it was close to 1.2 million.[5]

—*Surge of immigration.* A significant expansion has also occurred in the number of people obtaining legal permanent resident status in the United States. This number rose from 3.3 million in the 1960s to 9.5 million in just the first nine years of the new millennium, and this does not include the continued surge of illegal immigration.[6] These developments, too, have created increased demands for a variety of acculturation and resettlement services, not to mention related human and health services, that nonprofits have long provided.

—*Cultural subgroups.* Equally important is the emergence of at least one demographic subgroup that may hold some promise of helping the nonprofit sector meet some of this expanded demand. The subgroup in question is what demographers have termed "cultural creatives," an estimated 50 million people distinguished from others in the population by their preference for holistic thinking, their cosmopolitanism, their social activism, and their insistence on finding a better balance between work and personal values than the two other prominent population groups in American society, the "moderns" and the "traditionalists," seem to have found.[7] Though they have yet to develop a full self-consciousness, cultural creatives are powerfully attracted to the mission orientation of the nonprofit sector and could well help resolve some of the sector's human resource challenges.

Taken together, these and other sociodemographic changes have expanded the demand for many of the services that nonprofit organizations have traditionally provided, such as child day care, home health and nursing home care for the elderly, family counseling, foster care, relocation assistance, and substance abuse treatment and prevention. The demand for these services has spread well beyond the poor, moreover, and now encompasses middle-class households with resources to pay for them, a phenomenon that one analyst calls "the transformation of social services."[8] The foster care system alone, for example, has ballooned, as the number of children in foster care doubled between the early 1980s and the early 1990s, though the growth subsided somewhat in the new millennium. At the same time, the welfare reform legislation enacted in 1996, with its stress on job readiness, has created additional demand for the services that nonprofits typically offer.

While these demographic developments have increased the demand for nonprofit services, they may also be contributing to the supply of personnel willing to help meet this demand, as the growing elderly population cycles out of full-time work and into greater volunteer involvement and as cultural creatives find in the nonprofit sector a combination of work and meaning that fulfills their own sense of worth.

Greater Visibility and Policy Salience

Another factor working to the advantage of nonprofit organizations has been a spate of political and policy developments that has substantially increased the visibility of these organizations. This has included the neoliberal ideology popularized in the 1980s by Margaret Thatcher in the United Kingdom and Ronald Reagan in the United States with their antigovernment rhetoric and their emphasis on philanthropy and the private sector, including the private nonprofit sector, as better vehicles than government for addressing human needs; the revival of these notions with the rise of the Tea Party movement in the United States in 2008 and beyond, despite the evidence of for-profit excesses that produced the 2008 economic crisis; the significant credibility that the concept of "civil society," of citizen self-organization, gained during the uprisings that brought down communism in central Europe in the latter 1980s and again in the citizen movements challenging authoritarian regimes in the Arab Spring of 2011; the recent emphasis on the importance of "social capital" in promoting democracy and economic growth and the linkage of social capital to the presence of associations;[9] the growing enthusiasm over the emergence of "social entrepreneurs" and the "social ventures" they are creating; and the Obama administration's support for social innovation and the social entrepreneurs that promote it.

Responding to the buzz surrounding civil society and the nonprofit sector, the academic community has taken a newfound interest in these organizations. Research centers focusing on nonprofit organizations and philanthropy have been established at such institutions as Yale University, Johns Hopkins University, Indiana University, Harvard University, and the Urban Institute beginning as early as 1975 and extending into the 1990s and beyond. In addition, nonprofit studies has slowly penetrated the academic curriculum. As of 2009, 168 U.S. colleges or universities had graduate degree programs with a concentration in the operation of nonprofit organizations, up from only 17 as recently as 1990.[10] Despite the evidence of declining confidence in nonprofit organizations, moreover, other evidence points to continued popular support. Public opinion polls thus reveal continued widespread involvement in charitable giving and volunteering, key supports for the country's nonprofit organizations.[11] What is more, a robust set of infrastructure organizations has grown up to support various types of nonprofit organizations and the nonprofit field as a whole.[12]

New Technology

A third factor at least potentially of assistance to the nonprofit sector is the extraordinary array of technological advances that has become available thanks to the communications and biotechnology revolutions of the past several decades. To be sure, as noted in the prior chapter, technology is a two-edged sword for the nonprofit sector. On the one hand, it poses challenges to nonprofits because of its associated capital requirements. But as labor-intensive organizations, nonprofits stand to benefit greatly from the technology revolution if they can find the resources of capital and knowledge to do so. "Distributed learning" that provides new options for small liberal arts colleges, the promotion of newly developed green technologies by nonprofit environmental organizations, "social networking civic activism" to transform nonprofit advocacy, and developments in biosciences that could revolutionize medical treatment in nonprofit hospitals and clinics are just some of the opportunities that new technologies offer to nonprofits.[13]

The New Philanthropy

Also working to the benefit of the nonprofit sector is a series of developments affecting private philanthropy. These include the following:

—A widely anticipated *intergenerational transfer of wealth* between the baby boom generation and its offspring over the next twenty to thirty years, though the sharp drop in home prices beginning in 2008 and the rising cost of health care for the baby boom generation seem likely to take a large bite out of this rather optimistic scenario.[14]

—The greater corporate willingness to engage in partnerships and collaborations with nonprofit organizations, which has resulted from globalization and the resulting importance of corporate "reputational capital."[15]

—The dot.com phenomenon, which led to the accumulation of enormous fortunes in the hands of a small group of high-tech entrepreneurs, some of whom have turned their newfound wealth into charitable activities.[16]

—The parallel emergence of a robust group of social entrepreneurs who are finding new ways to use business means to serve social ends and an inventive group of philanthropists and social investors who are developing new tools through which to leverage private investment capital and channel it into social ventures and social and environmental purposes.[17]

Together, these developments are injecting a substantial amount of new blood and new energy into the philanthropic field, creating new opportunities for meeting the nonprofit sector's capital, talent, and reputational needs.

Summary

In short, American nonprofit organizations have not only been buffeted by a variety of significant challenges. They have also enjoyed a number of important opportunities. What is really important, however, is not just the scope of these competing pressures, but how the organizations have responded. It is to this topic that we therefore now turn.

6

The Nonprofit Response:
A Story of Resilience

How has nonprofit America responded to the extraordinary combination of challenges and opportunities it has faced over the past several decades? Has the sector been able to cope with the challenges and take advantage of the opportunities? And with what consequences for its current health and character and for its likely evolution? More significantly, have the responses advantaged any of the four impulses identified earlier, and if so, what implications does this have for the role that nonprofits are likely to play in national life?

The answers to these questions are especially important in light of the conventional wisdom about the responsiveness of nonprofit organizations. "Profit-making organizations are more flexible with respect to the deployment and redeployment of resources," management experts Rosabeth Kanter and David Summers wrote in 1987. "But the centrality of mission for nonprofit organizations places limitations on their flexibility of action."[1] Nonprofits are not to be trusted, Regina Herzlinger similarly explained to readers of the *Harvard Business Review* in 1996, because they lack the three basic accountability measures that ensure effective and efficient business operations: the self-interest of owners, competition, and the ultimate bottom-line measure of profitability.[2]

Contrary to these conventional beliefs, however, nonprofit America has responded with striking resilience to the complex challenges and opportunities it has recently confronted and continues to confront. Though largely unheralded, nonprofit America has undergone a quiet revolution during this period, a massive process of reinvention and reengineering that is still under way. To be sure, the resulting changes are hardly universal. What is more, there are serious questions about whether the resulting changes are in a wholly desirable direction or whether they have exposed the sector to unacceptable risks. While important shadings are needed to do justice to the considerable diversity that exists, there is no denying the dominant picture of resilience, adaptation, and change. More specifically, four broad threads of change are apparent.

Overall Sector Growth

In the first place, despite the cutbacks of the early 1980s, nonprofit organizations registered substantial growth over the thirty years between 1977 and 2007. What is more, although that growth slowed considerably with the onset of the 2008 financial crisis and ensuing recession, nonprofit revenue continued to grow faster than the overall economy even during this period. Thus, as figure 6-1 shows, between 1977 and 1996 nonprofit revenues swelled by 96 percent after adjusting for inflation, for an average annual growth rate of 3.6 percent. By comparison, during this same period the GDP grew by a significantly smaller 3.0 percent a year. Put somewhat differently, nonprofit revenues increased at a rate that was 20 percent faster than the overall U.S. GDP.[3]

What is more, this growth was not restricted only to nonprofit health organizations. Rather, while nonprofit health organizations boosted their revenue by 109 percent between 1977 and 1996, nonprofit arts organi-

Figure 6-1.   *Average Annual Change in Nonprofit Service and Expressive Organization Revenues vs. GDP, 1977–2011, Adjusted for Inflation*

Percent change in GDP and nonprofit revenue

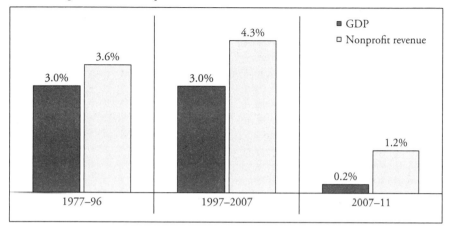

Source: 2007–11: NP revenue data from IRS microdata; price index for NPISH, BEA table 1.9.4; GDP data from NIPA table 1.3.6, Real Gross Value Added by Sector, Chained Dollars. All other periods: figure 1.6 in Lester M. Salamon, ed., *The State of Nonprofit America*, 2nd ed. (Brookings, 2012). For further detail, see chapter 6, note 3.

zations grew by 114 percent and nonprofit social service organizations by 117 percent.[4]

But the growth in nonprofit revenue accelerated even further in the more recent 1997–2007 period. Thus, as figure 6-1 also shows, during the ten years between 1997 and 2007 nonprofit revenues grew by another 53 percent after adjusting for inflation, for an average growth rate of 4.3 percent a year, well above its 3.6 percent growth rate in the earlier 1977–96 period and substantially higher than the overall 3.0 percent average annual growth rate of the U.S. economy during the same period.

As figure 6-2 shows, this more recent growth, too, was not restricted to any one component of the nonprofit sector. Although the category of "other" organizations—civic, international, and other—appears to have surged ahead of other fields, this is likely a reflection of the small base against which these percentages are computed. More generally, the annual growth of most substantial fields of nonprofit activity (health, education, social services) hovered around 4 percent during this 1997–2007 period,

Figure 6-2.   *Average Annual Change in Nonprofit Service and Expressive Organization Revenues, by Field, 1997–2007 vs. 2007–11, Inflation Adjusted*

Percent change in nonprofit revenue

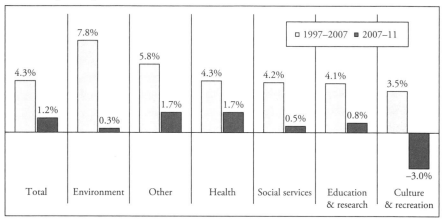

Source: See figure 6-1 and chapter 6, note 3.

and the one laggard—culture and recreation—still had a growth rate (3.5 percent) that beat that of the U.S. GDP.

While the *rate* of growth in the nonprofit sector was quite uniform across components, the share of the growth captured by the various segments differed markedly, reflecting the divergent scale of these segments. Thus health care nonprofits generated 57 percent of the growth of the nonprofit sector between 1997 and 2007, roughly equivalent to the share of the total with which they started the period. Education organizations accounted for 21 percent of the growth, and social service providers, 14 percent. The remaining organizations—culture and recreation, environment, and international—accounted for the remaining 8 percent.

Evidence of the vibrancy of the nonprofit sector extends well beyond financial indicators, however, which are heavily influenced by the performance of the largest organizations. Equally revealing is the record of organizational formation. Between 1977 and 1997 the number of 501(c)(3) and 501(c)(4) organizations registered with the Internal Revenue Service increased by 115 percent, or about 23,000 organizations a year.[5] By comparison, the number of business organizations increased by only 76 percent during this same period. The rate of nonprofit organization formation seems to have accelerated in more recent years, moreover, jumping to an average of 45,000 a year between 1997 and 2009, and this despite increased pressures for organizational mergers and the onset of the 2007–09 recession. Evidently, Americans are still finding in the nonprofit sector a convenient outlet for a wide assortment of social, economic, political, and cultural concerns.[6]

As figure 6-1 shows, however, during the post–2008 financial crisis period, the growth rate of nonprofit revenue slowed considerably, to an annual average of 1.2 percent per year between 2007 and 2011 (the latest date for which reliable data are available as of this writing). Even so, revenue growth remained positive overall during this period and outdistanced the growth rate of the economy as a whole by a factor of 6:1. During this recent period, however, considerable disparities emerged in the revenue growth rates of different segments of the nonprofit sector, as seen in figure 6-2. In particular, the health segment, while experiencing considerably slower average growth than during the earlier periods, nevertheless outpaced the growth rates of nonprofit education and research organizations and of social service organizations by multiples of two or three. And nonprofits in the field of arts and culture suffered an actual decline that averaged 3 percent a year.

Commercialization

What accounts for this prior record of robust growth, and how has it been affected by the recent recession? While many factors have played a part, the dominant one during the prior periods appears to be the vigor with which nonprofit America embraced the spirit and techniques of the market. The impact of the commercial and managerial impulse on the nonprofit sector increased enormously over the past two decades and manifested itself in a number of ways. During the post–financial crisis period, however, it has been government funding that allowed the nonprofit sector and those it serves to avoid a more calamitous collapse.

Growth of Commercial Income

Perhaps the clearest indication of the penetration of the commercial impulse into nonprofit operations has been the substantial rise in nonprofit commercial income, that is, income from service fees, investment earnings, and sales of products.[7] This reflects the success with which nonprofit organizations took advantage of the demographic trends noted above by marketing their services to a clientele both increasingly in need of nonprofit services and able to pay for them. In fact, nonprofit income from these commercial sources surged 64 percent in real dollar terms between 1997 and 2007, accounting in the process for nearly 60 percent of the sector's revenue growth during this period—twice as much as its nearest competitor. In the process, commercial income strengthened its position as the dominant source of nonprofit service and expressive organization revenue, with 57.5 percent of the total as of 2007.

Fees and other commercial sources of nonprofit income not only grew in overall scale but also spread to ever-broader components of the sector. Already dominant in health, higher education, and the arts by 1997, commercial income extended its reach to other areas of nonprofit activity as well. Thus, for example, as figure 6-3 shows, commercial income also accounted for 40 percent of the revenue growth of nonprofit social service organizations during the 1997–2007 period. Even religious organizations

Figure 6-3. *Sources of Nonprofit Revenue Growth, by Field, 1997–2007*

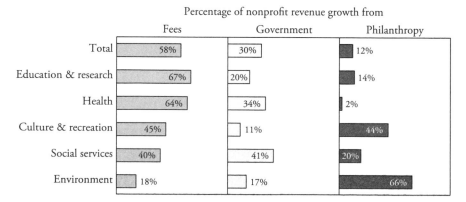

Source: See figure 6-1 and chapter 6, note 3.

boosted their commercial income during this period, largely through the sale or rental of church property.[8]

In only one field—culture and recreation—did the commercial tide weaken during the 1997–2007 period. While fees and charges remained the largest source of revenue growth for culture and recreation organizations, as they did for the nonprofit sector as a whole between 1997 and 2007, that dominance actually slipped somewhat for this segment of the sector. Thus, while fees and charges accounted for 57 percent of the income of these organizations as of 1997, they accounted for a much smaller 45 percent of the revenue growth between 1997 and 2007, as culture and recreation organizations, feeling some pushback from patrons, made a concerted effort to boost their philanthropic support instead. As we will see below, this strategy did not pay off well for culture and arts organizations during the early post–financial crisis period.

To secure such commercial income, nonprofits have naturally had to go where the "customers" are, which has meant a migration of nonprofit jobs to the suburbs and the Sun Belt. This is evident in the growing suburbanization of philanthropy that occurred during the 1980s and in the geographic spread of nonprofit employment.[9] Seventy percent of the substantial growth of nonprofit employment in the state of Maryland between 1989 and 1999, for example, took place in the Baltimore and Washington suburbs, whereas the city of Baltimore, which started the period with nearly half of the state's nonprofit employment, accounted for only 17 percent of the growth between 1989 and 1999. This pattern has continued into more recent years as well. Thus the Baltimore and Washington suburbs, with 53 percent of the state's nonprofit employment as of 2008, accounted for 58 percent of the state's nonprofit employment growth between 2008 and 2010, while the city of Baltimore, with 37 percent of the nonprofit jobs, accounted for a much smaller 29 percent of the nonprofit job growth.[10]

This overall pattern of nonprofit revenue growth slowed dramatically, however, in the wake of the 2008 financial crisis and the ensuing recession. For one thing, as already noted, while nonprofit revenue continued to grow, the rate of growth dropped fairly sharply, to a scant 1.2 percent per year of average growth. As of 2011, therefore, nonprofit revenue had risen only $72 billion over its 2007 level, a mere 5 percent of its nearly $1.5 trillion base.

Perhaps more discouragingly, private giving as of 2011 remained approximately $3 billion below its 2007 level. This means that the other two major sources of support actually added approximately $75 billion to the net total, with $3 billion going to fill the hole left by the decline in charitable support.

Interestingly, as noted in figure 6-4, of this gross increase, 79 percent was provided by government and only 21 percent by fees and charges, reversing a pattern that spanned the previous several decades. This likely reflects the impact of the "safety net" government entitlement programs, particularly Medicare and Medicaid, as well as of the stimulus program sponsored and pushed by the incoming Obama administration.

Reflecting this, nonprofit health organizations captured over 60 percent of the increased government funding made available to nonprofits as of 2011, with education claiming 17 percent and social services about

Figure 6-4.   *Sources of Increase in Nonprofit Revenue, 2007–11,*
Constant 2011 Dollars

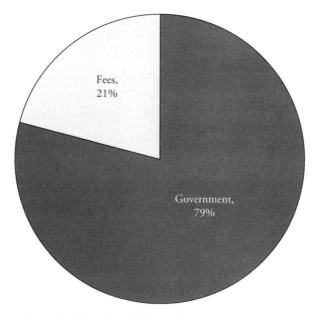

Fees, 21%

Government, 79%

Source: See figure 6-1 and chapter 6, note 3.

Table 6-1. *Sources of Nonprofit Revenue, 2011 vs. 2007*

Source	2007	2011
Government	32.5%	34.8%
Philanthropy	10.0%	9.4%
Fees, dividends	57.5%	55.8%
TOTAL	100.0%	100.0%

Source: See figure 6-1 and chapter 6, note 3.

12 percent. Clearly, government financial support saved significant components of the nonprofit sector from a much more serious disaster during this period. By contrast, fee income declined for social service, arts, environmental, and civic organizations, while philanthropic support remained flat for social service organizations and suffered reductions for arts, education, and environmental organizations.

Reflecting these shifts, the funding base of the nonprofit sector changed somewhat as a result of the financial crisis and ensuing recession. In particular, as reflected in table 6-1, the government share of overall nonprofit revenue increased from 32.5 percent to 34.8 percent while both the fee and philanthropy portions declined.

Adaptation to the New Terrain of Public Funding

As these recent post–financial crisis changes make clear, nonprofits seem to have adapted well to the recent changes in the tools of action through which government assistance is reaching them. Indeed, this is another reflection of the commercialization of the nonprofit sector, since the terrain of public funding has itself grown more commercial as a consequence of the shift to consumer-side subsidies discussed earlier. Despite this shift, nonprofits managed to boost their government support 195 percent in real dollar terms between 1977 and 1997. Government support accounted for 42 percent of the nonprofit service and expressive organizations' substantial growth during this period as a consequence.

Behind these numbers lie some creative nonprofit responses to the enormous shifts in the forms of public sector support. Social service agencies had to be particularly nimble in adjusting to the new realities, as states shifted their social service spending from stagnant or declining discretionary grant programs to the rapidly growing Medicaid and Supplemental Security Income (SSI) programs, both of which deliver their benefits to clients and therefore require agencies to master new marketing, billing, and reimbursement-management skills. Similarly impressive is the success of nonprofit housing and community development organizations in taking advantage of the new Low-Income Housing Tax Credit program designed to stimulate the flow of private investment capital into low-income housing.[11]

The overall growth of nonprofit revenue from government slowed somewhat in the 1997–2007 period, however, during which government support to nonprofit organizations, including through Medicaid and Medicare, increased by 38 percent, well below the 53 percent rate of growth of overall nonprofit revenue. Government support thus accounted for a considerably smaller 30 percent of the sector's overall growth. This was largely due, however, to the cost-control measures introduced into the huge Medicare and Medicaid programs. Outside of health care providers, the growth in government support to nonprofit organizations during the 1997–2007 period has been substantial—149 percent for environmental organizations, 82 percent for education organizations, 69 percent for social assistance organizations, and 61 percent for international assistance organizations. This growth attests to the success many nonprofit organizations achieved in adapting to the changes in the structure of government funding streams by repackaging traditional social services as behavioral health services and securing government support through the expanding health programs. At the same time, because the government share of total income is somewhat small for some of these fields (for example, arts and culture), the government contribution to overall revenue growth in a number of these fields remained limited despite the percentage growth that occurred.

The significant expansion of government support, particularly in health and social services, has had its downsides, of course. Particularly problematic is the tendency for Medicaid (and to some extent Medicare) reimbursement rates to fall behind the actual costs of delivering the services they are intended to support.[12] For-profit vendors can respond to these cuts by pulling out of the affected lines of business, but nonprofits often find this difficult. As a consequence, nonprofit organizations often end up subsidizing, with scarce private charitable resources, services they have undertaken to help fulfill federal program priorities.

Even so, the success with which nonprofit organizations have adapted to the new government funding realities is another indication of the penetration of the commercial impulse into the nonprofit sector, since so much of government aid now takes the form of consumer-side subsidies. When this voucher-type government support is added to the fee income that nonprofits received in 2007 (as it is in the data on "program service revenue" that nonprofit organizations report to the Internal Revenue Service on their 990 forms), it turns out that 81 percent of the reported income of nonprofit 501(c)(3) organizations, exclusive of churches, shows up as commercial or quasi-commercial revenue. Even among nonprofits in the social service field, the combination of consumer-side government subsidies and fee income accounted for three-fifths (61 percent) of total revenue in 2007. And this pattern merely expanded during the post–financial crisis period.

Expanded Venture Activity

A third manifestation of the penetration of commercial impulses into the nonprofit sector is the sector's increased involvement in commercial ventures. Such ventures differ from the collection of fees for standard nonprofit services in that they entail the creation and sale of products and services primarily for a commercial market. Examples include museum gift shops and online stores, church rentals of social halls, licensing agreements between research universities and commercial firms, and, in recent years, the growth of so-called social ventures—that is, organizations that pursue their social or environmental missions through businesses that generate revenues from the sale of goods or services.

Existing law has long allowed nonprofit organizations to engage in commercial activities as long as these activities do not become the primary purpose of the organization. Since 1951 the income from such ventures has been subject to corporate income taxation unless it is "related" to the charitable purpose of the organization.

Solid data on the scope of this activity are difficult to locate, however, since much of it is considered "related" income and buried in the statistics on fees, but the clear impression from what data exist suggests a substantial expansion over the past two decades. One sign of this is the growth in so-called unrelated business income reported to the Internal Revenue Service. Although the IRS is notoriously liberal in its definition of what constitutes "related," as opposed to "unrelated," business income, the number of charities reporting such income increased by 35 percent between 1990 and 1997, and the amount of income they reported more than doubled.[13] In 1997 gross unrelated business income reported by all types of nonprofit organizations reached $7.8 billion, an increase of 7 percent over the previous year—and following even larger percentage increases over the previous two years. Much of this income flows to member-serving nonprofits, but 501(c)(3) and 501(c)(4) organizations accounted for 57 percent of it. The unrelated business activity of nonprofits grew even further in recent years. Thus the number of 501(c)(3) and 501(c)(4) organizations reporting such unrelated business income increased by another 32 percent between 1997 and 2007, and the value of their earnings increased by nearly 25 percent after adjusting for inflation.[14] Still, only about 5 percent of all charitable nonprofits reported any unrelated business income in 2007, and for most of those that did, the deductions taken against this income came very close to balancing out the income earned, suggesting either that such enterprises are not very "profitable" or that nonprofits have learned how to allocate expenses so as to minimize tax obligations.

Far more widespread than "unrelated" business activity in the nonprofit sphere is the "related" business activity that many nonprofits are undertaking. Cultural institutions seem to be especially inventive in adapting venture activities to their operations, perhaps because they have the clearest "products" to sell. The Guggenheim Museum has even gone global, with franchises in Italy, Germany, and Spain, while elaborate touring exhibitions and shows have become standard facets of museum, orchestra, and dance company operations. Cultural institutions also actively exploit the new digitization technologies, often in collaboration with commercial firms. In the process, arts organizations are being transformed from inward-oriented institutions focused primarily on their collections to outward-oriented enterprises competing for customers in an increasingly commercial market, though this enthusiasm has encountered some pushback in the arts world.[15] The latest craze is the marketing not of products—reproductions of paintings or coffee mugs with Chagall's Bible scenes—but digitized artistic expressions and momentary artistic interactions delivered through mobile devices.[16]

Other types of nonprofit organizations are also increasingly involved in commercial-type ventures. Thus hospitals are investing in parking garages, universities establishing joint ventures with private biotechnology companies, and social service agencies operating managed care and crisis intervention businesses financed by corporate customers.[17] The business activities of nonprofit hospitals have grown especially complex, with elaborate purchasing and marketing consortia linking hospitals, medical practitioners, insurance groups, and equipment suppliers.[18]

Perhaps the most interesting facet of this venture activity in the nonprofit arena, however, is the recent tendency of some nonprofit organizations to utilize business ventures not simply to generate income but to carry out their basic charitable missions.[19] This reflects the broader transformation in prevailing conceptions of how to address poverty, from one focused on providing services to one focused on providing jobs. Thus, rather than merely training disadvantaged individuals and sending them out into the private labor market, a new class of social purpose enterprises, or social ventures, has emerged to employ former drug addicts, inmates, or other disadvantaged persons in actual businesses as a way to build skills, develop self-confidence, and teach work habits. Other such ventures are manufacturing and distributing products or services that ease environmental pollution, overcome disabilities, or serve other social or environmental purposes. Examples here include the Greyston Bakery in Yonkers, New York, which trains and hires unemployable workers in its gourmet bakery business; Pioneer Human Services, a nonprofit in Seattle, Washington, that operates an aircraft parts manufacturing facility, food buying and warehousing services, and restaurants that employ disadvantaged workers and prepare them for the labor market; and Bikeable Communities in Long Beach, California, which promotes bicycle use by offering valet and related services to cyclists.[20] The result is a thoroughgoing marriage of market means to charitable purpose and the emergence of a new, hybrid form of nonprofit business.

The emergence and expansion of social enterprises has also brought with it a significant degree of institutional innovation in the nonprofit arena. Because social enterprise managers have found their expansion constrained by the lack of access that nonprofit organizations have to the equity markets to generate capital, and because for-profit companies are bound by law to maximize profits instead of pursuing social purposes, social entrepreneurs have begun experimenting with a variety of "flexible purpose" corporate forms. Thus, for example, ten states have adopted statutes permitting the formation of so-called L3Cs, or low-profit limited liability companies, and other innovative hybrid forms are being actively explored, though the expansion of the L3C form has apparently stalled.[21]

Taken together, these developments have created a certain buzz in the nonprofit and social-purpose arena, as social entrepreneurs and the social enterprises they create have become the change agents of the new millennium, displacing traditional nonprofit managers as role models for socially and environmentally oriented activists. The award of the Nobel Peace Prize to the social entrepreneur Muhammad Yunus in 2006; the appearance of books on social enterprise with titles such as *How to Change the World, The Fortune at the Bottom of the Pyramid,* and *The Power of Social Innovation;* and the creation of a Social Innovation Fund in the early days of the Obama administration provide evidence of the energy and enthusiasm this movement has unleashed.[22]

Managerial Professionalism

A fourth manifestation of the commercial impulse in the nonprofit sector is the growing professionalization of nonprofit operations. Professionalization may be too blanket a term to depict the recent shifts in the staffing and operation of nonprofit organizations, however, for it has at least three different meanings. The first is the basic expansion of paid staff, not necessarily replacing volunteers but certainly displacing them as the backbone of nonprofit operations. Though volunteers continue to play important roles in the nonprofit sector, the myth that portrays these organizations as principally operated by volunteers now no longer comes close to describing reality, at least for the bulk of nonprofit activity if not for the bulk of the organizations. In point of fact, nonprofit organizations had become major employers by the late 1970s, and their attraction of paid staff has continued into the new century. Indeed, between the late 1970s and the mid-1990s, the paid staff of nonprofit organizations grew at an annual rate more than 70 percent higher than that of all nonagricultural employment.[23] This disparity in employment growth has not only continued but has accelerated in the new millennium, as the U.S. economy continues its structural shift from manufacturing to services. Thus nonprofit employment grew two and one-half times faster than overall nonfarm employment between 1998 and 2005, and it sustained this growth through much of the economic recession of 2008 and beyond.[24] In fact, the rate of growth of nonprofit employment exceeded that of for-profit employment in every year but one in the first decade of the twenty-first century, and in that year the two tied.[25] Indeed, if the nonprofit sector were itself one of the eighteen "industries" into which statisticians divide economies, as of 2007 it would be the third-largest such industry in the U.S. economy in terms of employment, behind only retail trade and manufacturing.

The second meaning of professionalization involves the penetration of subject-matter professionals into leadership positions in organizations. This, too, is an old story. As noted earlier, the professionalization of the health, education, and even social service spheres in this sense occurred fairly early in the twentieth century. This type of professionalization was a later arrival in the arts field, though it has had its characteristic results of creating an inward-looking performance culture, which stands accused of pushing contemporary composers to the sideline, constraining musical innovation, and losing touch with younger and more diverse audiences.[26] More generally, as one scholar notes, "Although some nonprofit industries, such as education and health care, had been professionally managed for decades, by the end of the Reagan era, professionalization had penetrated every area in which nonprofits operated, including religion."[27]

As noted earlier, however, the professionalism impulse has encountered significant resistance in recent years, and subject matter professionals have been put on the defensive. At the same time, a third, more commercial-oriented type of professionalism—managerial professionalism—has arisen to challenge subject-matter professionals.[28] Rather than substantive training in health, education, or casework, managerial professionals are trained in the techniques of rational management, such as strategic planning, management by objectives, segmentation of operations along individual lines of business, and the use of metrics. Indeed, substantive professionals are now increasingly being managed by managerial professionals, who hold them accountable for performance goals and productivity gains.

All of this suggests a broader and deeper penetration of the market culture into the fabric of nonprofit operations. Nonprofit organizations are increasingly marketing their "products," viewing their clients as "customers," "segmenting their markets," differentiating their output, identifying their "market niches," formulating business plans, and generally incorporating the language, and the style, of business management into the operation of their agencies. As one student of the field has remarked, nonprofit executives are now "among the most entrepreneurial managers to be found anywhere, including the private for-profit sector."[29]

How fully the culture of the market has been integrated into the operations, as opposed to the rhetoric, of the nonprofit sector is difficult to determine. However, a survey of a core set of nonprofit human service, arts, and community development organizations by the Johns Hopkins Listening Post Project finds widespread adoption of at least one aspect of the market mantra: the need for improved performance metrics, with 85 percent of surveyed agencies reporting measuring the performance of at least a portion of their programs and 70 percent reporting use of "outcome," and not just "output," measures.[30] Certainly the appetite for market-oriented materials has been robust enough to convince commercial publishers like John Wiley and Sons to invest heavily in the field, producing a booming market in how-to books offering nonprofit managers training in "strategic planning," "financial planning," "mission-based management," "social entrepreneurship," "street-smart financial basics," "strategic communications," "high-performance philanthropy," and "high-performance organization," to cite just a handful of recent titles.[31]

The Drucker Foundation's Self-Assessment Tool, with its market-oriented stress on the five questions considered most critical to nonprofit-organization performance (What is our mission? Who is our customer? What does the customer value? What are our results? What is our plan?), was reportedly purchased by more than 10,000 agencies in the first five years following its publication in 1993, and Mario Morino's *Leap of Reason,* preaching the gospel of "managing to outputs," claims 80,000 copies in circulation, suggesting the appetite for business-style management advice within the sector.[32] Illustrative of the penetration of market-oriented management tools into the nonprofit sector was the discovery by researchers in San Francisco of a management training session for aspiring ministers featuring a PowerPoint presentation entitled "Building Market Share for Jesus."[33]

That the market culture is changing organizational practices, organizational structures, and interorganizational behavior is evident even in the most voluntaristic components of the nonprofit field, including, for example, charitable giving. A veritable revolution has occurred in this arena of nonprofit action, as reflected in the emergence and growth of specialized fundraising organizations, such as the National Society of Fund Raising Executives (1960), now the Association of Fundraising Professionals (AFP); the Council for Advancement and Support of Education (1974); the Association for Healthcare Philanthropy (1967); and the National Committee on Planned Giving (1988), now the Partnership for Philanthropic Planning. As recently as 1979, the AFP, the largest of these organizations, boasted only 1,899 members. By 2011 it claimed over 30,000 members in 230 chapters around the globe.[34] Equally impressive has been the transformation in the technology of charitable giving through the development of such devices as workplace solicitation, telethons, direct-mail campaigns, telephone solicitation, complex planned-giving vehicles such as charitable remainder trusts, and, more recently, e-philanthropy.

Entire organizations have surfaced to manage this process of extracting funds, including charitable funds originated by for-profit investment firms such as Fidelity Investments, providing investors an opportunity to manage their charitable resources through a nonprofit closely allied with the firm that handles their regular investments.[35]

Also notable is the emergence in philanthropic space of a host of new actors who are focused on channeling private investment capital from banks, insurance companies, pension funds, and high-net-worth individuals into social-purpose activities. Included here are entities known by such nontraditional charitable terms as capital aggregators, social-purpose secondary markets, social stock exchanges, enterprise brokers, and foundations as philanthropic banks, all of them using financial instruments that go well beyond the normal mechanism of the charitable grant.[36] How successfully these developments will withstand the effects of the recent economic turmoil remains to be seen, but they have clearly established a beachhead that augurs well for their future.

These developments in the field of fundraising hardly begin to exhaust the changes in organizational behavior and structure ushered into the nonprofit field by the powerful commercial and managerial impulse. Hospitals, for example, are increasingly advertising their capabilities, universities investing in off-campus programs, museums and symphonies establishing venues in shopping centers, and even small community development organizations engaging in complex real estate syndications. Significant changes are also occurring in the basic structure and governance of nonprofit organizations. Boards are being made smaller and more selective, substituting a corporate model for a community-based one. Similarly, greater efforts are being made to recruit business leaders to serve on boards, further solidifying the dominant corporate culture. In addition, the internal structure of organizations is growing more complex. To some extent this is driven by prevailing legal restrictions. Thus, many nonprofit advocacy organizations have created 501(c)(4) subsidiaries to bypass restrictions on their lobbying activity as 501(c)(3) charities.[37] Similarly, nonprofit residential care facilities are segmenting their various activities into separate corporate entities to build legal walls around core operations in case of liability challenges. And universities, freed by the Bayh-Dole Act and subsequent legislation to patent discoveries developed with federal research funds, are turning to complex consortium arrangements to market the products of university-based scientific research.[38]

Behind the comforting image of relatively homey charities, nonprofit organizations are thus being transformed into complex holding companies, with multiple nonprofit and for-profit subsidiaries and offshoots, significantly complicating the task of operational and financial management and control. Not surprisingly, to cope with this increased complexity, nonprofit management has had to become increasingly professional. These developments have thus helped to fuel the growth of the new nonprofit management training programs mentioned earlier, 168 of which were in existence in colleges and universities across the country as of 2009.[39] Other evidence of the growing managerial professionalization of the nonprofit field includes the construction of a set of sector-wide infrastructure institutions, such as Independent Sector, the Council on Foundations, the Association of Small Foundations, the Forum of Regional Associations of Grantmakers, and state nonprofit organizations; as well as the emergence of a nonprofit press that includes the *Chronicle of Philanthropy*, *NonProfit Times*, *Nonprofit Quarterly*, and *Stanford Social Innovation Review*.[40]

What was once a scatteration of largely overlooked institutions has thus become a booming cottage industry, attracting organizations, personnel, publications, services, conferences, websites, head-hunting firms, consultants, rituals, and fads—all premised on the proposition that nonprofit organizations are distinctive institutions with enough commonalities, despite their many differences, to be studied, represented, serviced, trained, and, most important, managed using a similar set of concepts and tools, but a set inspired in important part by those in use in the business sector.

New Business Partnerships

As the culture of the market has spread into the fabric of nonprofit operations, old suspicions between the nonprofit and business sectors have significantly softened, opening the way for nonprofit acceptance of the business community not simply as a source of charitable support but as a legitimate partner for a wide range of nonprofit endeavors. This perspective has been championed by charismatic sector leaders such as Billy Shore who urge nonprofits to stop thinking about how to get donations and start thinking about how to "market" the considerable "assets" they control, including particularly the asset represented by their reputations.[41] This has meshed nicely with the growing readiness of businesses to forge strategic alliances with nonprofits in order to generate "reputational capital," demonstrating that the penetration of the business culture into the nonprofit sector has been accompanied by a significant penetration of the nonprofit culture into business operations, as businesses have begun developing mission statements and aligning products with good causes. The upshot has been a notable upsurge in strategic partnerships between nonprofit organizations and businesses.

One early manifestation of this was American Express's invention of "cause-related marketing" in the early 1980s. Under this technique, a nonprofit lends its name to a commercial product in return for a share of the proceeds from the sale of that product. Research demonstrates that such arrangements bring substantial returns to the companies involved, boosting sales, enhancing company reputations, and buoying employee morale. Coca-Cola, for example, experienced a 490 percent spurt in the sales of its products at 450 Wal-Mart stores in 1997 when it launched a campaign promising to donate 15 cents to Mothers Against Drunk Driving for every soft-drink case it sold. More generally, a 1999 Cone/Roper survey found that two-thirds of Americans have greater trust in companies aligned with a social issue and that more than half of all workers wish their employers would do more to support social causes. This evidence has convinced a growing number of corporations to associate themselves and their products with social causes and the groups actively working on them. Thus, the apparel retailer Eddie Bauer has entered cause-related marketing arrangements with American Forests, Evian with Bill Shore's Share Our Strength, Liz Claiborne with the Family Violence Prevention Fund, Mattel with Girls Incorporated, Timberland with City Year, Yoplait with Susan G. Komen for the Cure, and many more. Indeed,

an entire cottage industry has sprung up around cause-related marketing, including the web-based Cause Marketing Forum, the website on-
Philanthropy.com for "professionals working on the social commons,"
and regular tracking of cause-related marketing proceeds by marketing
research firm IEG, LLC. By 2010 cause sponsorship was delivering an
estimated $1.62 billion in proceeds to nonprofit organizations, up from
$120 million in 2002.[42]

Increasingly, moreover, cause-related marketing relationships have
evolved into broader partnerships that mobilize corporate personnel, fi-
nances, and know-how in support of nonprofit activities. The most successful of these efforts deliver benefits to both the corporation and the
nonprofit. Thus, for example, when the Swiss pharmaceutical manufac-
turer Novartis contributed $25 million to the University of California at
Berkeley for basic biological research, it secured in the bargain the right
to negotiate licenses on a third of the discoveries of the school's Department of Plant and Microbial Biology, whether it paid for these discoveries or not.[43] The management expert Rosabeth Kanter even argues that
businesses are coming to see nonprofits not simply as sources of good corporate images but also as the "beta site for business innovation," a locus
for developing new approaches to long-standing business problems, such
as how to recruit inner-city customers to the banking system and how to
locate and train entry-level personnel for central-city hotels.[44] In these
and countless other ways nonprofit organizations and businesses have
begun reaching out to each other across historic divides of suspicion to
forge interesting collaborations of value to both, leading the Aspen Institute's Nonprofit Sector Strategy Group to "applaud the new strategic
approach that businesses are bringing to societal problem-solving and the
expansion of business partnerships with nonprofit groups to which it has
given rise."[45]

In short, a massive and multifaceted commercial surge has enveloped
the country's nonprofit sector, affecting its internal operation, its revenue base, its organizational structure, and its entire modus operandi.

Meeting the For-Profit Competition

One interesting consequence of the nonprofit absorption of the market culture is an enhanced capacity of nonprofits to hold their own in the face of the rising tide of for-profit competition. To be sure, the credit for this does not belong to nonprofits alone. Rather, the for-profit sector has proved to be far less formidable a competitor in many of the spheres in which both operate than initially seemed to be the case. As Bradford Gray and Mark Schlesinger point out, a "life-cycle" perspective is needed to understand the competitive relationship between nonprofit and for-profit organizations in the health field, and a similar observation very likely applies to other fields as well.[46] For-profit firms have distinct advantages during growth spurts in the life cycles of particular fields, when new services are in demand as a result either of changes in government policy or of shifting consumer needs. This is so because these firms can more readily access the capital markets to build new facilities, acquire new technology, and attract sophisticated management. In addition, they are better equipped to market their services and achieve the scale required to negotiate favorable terms with suppliers (for example, pharmaceutical companies).

However, once they become heavily leveraged, the continued success of these enterprises comes to depend on the expectation of continuing escalation of their stock prices. When this expectation is shaken, as it often is thanks to shifts in government policies—such as reimbursement policies for Medicare and Medicaid—the results can be catastrophic and precipitous. In such circumstances, for-profit firms can go bankrupt or exit particular fields—for example, by refusing to serve Medicaid recipients. In some cases they have also shown a distressing tendency to engage in fraudulent practices. In the 1990s, for example, some for-profit nursing homes, squeezed by new state policies designed to reduce Medicaid costs, turned to misleading billing practices to sustain their revenues and ultimately got caught. A similar scenario played out in the hospital field three times in the past several decades—first in the latter 1980s, again in the mid-1990s, and more recently in 2012. In each of these cases overly optimistic for-profit entrepreneurs found it impossible to sustain the growth paths that their stock valuations required and ended up being discredited when government agencies and private insurers found that they had fraudulently inflated their costs, overbilled for services, or employed inflated diagnoses to justify unduly complicated (and expensive) procedures.[47] This boom and bust cycle seems to operate as well in the social service field, particularly where government support is a crucial part of the demand structure of agencies. For-profit involvement grows in response to increased public funding but then suffers a shake-out when government reimbursement contracts.

All of this demonstrates why nonprofit involvement is so crucial, especially in fields where vulnerable populations are involved and the reliable maintenance of a basic level of quality care is essential. At the same time, such involvement is far from guaranteed, even where nonprofits pioneer the service. Given the intensity of competition at the present time, and the expanded access of for-profits to government support, nonprofits can hold their own only where they have well-established institutions, where they can secure capital, where they manage to identify a meaningful market niche and a distinctive product, where they respond effectively to the competitive threat, and where individual consumers or those who are paying on their behalf value the special qualities that the nonprofits bring to the field.[48] The fact that nonprofits have continued to expand substantially in the face of competition suggests that many nonprofits have been up to this challenge. What is more, the not-for-profit form is staging a renaissance in some unexpected places. One of these is the emergence of nonprofit, multispecialty physician groups, reflecting the reluctance of many young doctors, especially women, already burdened by heavy medical school debt, to take on the additional debt involved in opening their own practices or to handle the increasingly complex business dimensions of medical practice. One estimate is that a quarter of all practicing physicians now belong to such groups.[49] At the same time, recent reports indicating problems for nonprofit hospitals in generating capital to respond to a spurt in admissions make it clear that competitive challenges remain, even for quite large and sophisticated nonprofit providers.[50]

Sustaining an Advocacy Role

In addition to growing robustly, finding ways to market their services to paying customers, adjusting to a new terrain of government funding, and reengineering key features of their operations in response to the dominant market culture, American nonprofits have also demonstrated their resilience by maintaining a considerable presence in the realm of advocacy and citizen engagement. In this their performance stands in stark contrast to concerns about the decline of social capital and the disappearance of nationally integrated civic associations voiced by scholars such as Robert Putnam and Theda Skocpol.[51] One explanation for this lies in the impact of the communications revolution of the past two decades. Internet activism has fundamentally reshaped civic participation and advocacy, providing through social media, blogs, chat rooms, and other vehicles new ways for citizens to connect, share ideas, mobilize, and inform, as well as new ways for organizations to reach out to members and to form and manage advocacy coalitions.[52]

Also at work, however, is the professionalization of nonprofit advocacy activity. This was particularly evident during the period from the early 1960s through the early 1990s, perhaps the high point of nonprofit, public-interest advocacy involvement. During this period a variety of public interest advocacy groups effectively advanced agendas seeking improvements in civil rights, consumer protection, environmental protection, health care, and relief from hunger and poverty. As reflected in Jeffrey Berry's careful analysis of the role of such groups in shaping the congressional agenda during this period, though constituting only 7 percent of the Washington interest group universe throughout this period, these groups accounted for 24 to 32 percent of congressional testimony, generated 29 to 40 percent of the press coverage of pending legislation, and were nearly 80 percent as effective in passing legislation they favored as the business lobbies against which they were often arrayed.[53]

But nonprofit involvement in citizen engagement has persisted well beyond this period. Mainline civic and civil rights membership organizations, such as the League of Women Voters, the Jaycees, Kiwanis, the National Association for the Advancement of Colored People, the

National Council of La Raza, and the Urban League have now been joined by new organizations committed to strengthening democracy by promoting voting, civic participation, and community problem solving.

Citizen activism is particularly evident in the environmental area. Close to 680 watershed associations operate in the Chesapeake Bay watershed alone, for example, sampling water and checking for illegal discharges; and similar associations operate in other watersheds across the country, all of them linked together in the River Network. Land trusts, multi-stakeholder climate change and ecosystem partnerships, and environmental education coalitions fill out the rich organizational and associational tapestry of the contemporary environmental movement.[54] Beyond these citizen engagement activities, more traditional nonprofit advocacy organizations continue to grow. For example, the Sierra Club, a leading nonprofit environmental organization, boasted 1.3 million members in 2008–09, up from 246,000 in 1980, and other organizations are not far behind.[55]

In the process, nonprofit advocacy organizations have grown increasingly complex and professional. The Sierra Club, for example, is a 501(c)(4) organization that operates six other organizations: a legal defense fund, a foundation, a political action committee (PAC), a student coalition, a book club, and a property management company. In addition, it operates twenty-two regional offices, and chapters in every state. Nor is this type of development restricted to the environmental arena. The National Organization for Women (NOW)—like the Sierra Club a 501(c)(4) organization—also has a separate 501(c)(3) foundation, a number of PACs, a network of local chapters, and an active online presence through Facebook and Twitter.

More generally, research demonstrates that a sizable proportion of nonprofit service-providing organizations engage in some type of advocacy activity. Thus a 2000 survey of a cross section of nonprofit organizations found three-fourths reporting some engagement in public policy activity. This general finding was confirmed in a more recent survey by the Johns Hopkins Listening Post Project, which found that nearly three-quarters (73 percent) of a core set of human service, arts, and community development organization executives reported involvement in some type of policy advocacy or lobbying during the year leading up to the survey, with three out of five of these indicating some advocacy involvement almost every month.[56] This involvement is all the more impressive in light of the legal limitations on nonprofit political action—limitations that bar nonprofit organizations from engaging in electoral activity, from contributing to political campaigns, from devoting more than a limited share of their resources to lobbying, and from engaging in "political activity" if they receive government funds.[57]

Not only have nonprofit citizen groups proved effective in national political advocacy, but also they have extended their reach upward to the international level and downward to states and localities. The same new communications technologies that facilitated the rise of global corporations have permitted the emergence of transnational advocacy networks linking nonprofit citizen groups across national borders. This "third force" is rapidly transforming international politics and economics, challenging government policies on everything from land mines to dam construction and holding corporations to account in their home markets for environmental damage or labor practices they may be pursuing in far-off lands.[58] Indeed, the recent eagerness multinational corporations have shown for cause-related marketing arrangements and broader strategic partnerships with nonprofit organizations has been driven in important part by the threat these networks pose to these corporations' "license to operate" and to their reputations among both consumers and their own staff. Similarly, nonprofits have forged advocacy coalitions at the state level to make sure that devolution does not emasculate policy gains achieved nationally.

Impressive as the scope and scale of nonprofit involvement in civic engagement and advocacy may be, however, so too are its limitations. For one thing, lobbying and advocacy, while widespread and varied, tend to involve relatively limited commitments of time and resources for most organizations most of the time. Only about half of the organizations in the Johns Hopkins survey, for example, reported doing even the least-demanding forms of lobbying or advocacy during the year preceding the survey, and the proportions that were involved three or more times in the course of a year exceeded one-third of the organizations for only the least demanding of all forms (signing a correspondence to a government official).[59]

One reason for this fairly limited involvement appears to be the limited resources and resulting limited staff time available to support advocacy in most organizations. The vast majority (85 percent) of Listening Post Project respondents reported devoting less than 2 percent of their budgets to either lobbying or advocacy, and in most organizations the advocacy function is left largely to the executive director, with little effort to rally clients or patrons let alone engage other staff. Simple lack of resources was thus the most common barrier to greater policy engagement cited by respondents in both surveys cited above, outdistancing concerns about restrictive regulations by far, at least in the Johns Hopkins survey.[60]

Data on nonprofit expenditures on lobbying recorded on nonprofit Form 990 filings confirm these findings. Only 6,502 nonprofit 501(c)(3) organizations reported any lobbying expenditures in 2005, twice the number ten years earlier but still a mere 2 percent of all reporting organizations, and this despite the fact that all 501(c)(3) organizations are allowed to do some lobbying. What is more, the amount these organizations reported spending on lobbying remained below 0.1 percent of their total expenditures.[61] This pattern has certainly been true in the environmental arena. As Carmen Sirianni and Stephanie Sofer report, 40 percent of watershed groups sampled by the River Network had no budget, and three-fourths had no fundraising strategy. As a consequence, these groups lack the capability to engage substantial numbers of citizens for restoration efforts or to tackle the complex challenges of climate change, and similar problems confront land trusts and groups addressing toxics and environmental justice issues.[62]

Incredibly, and perhaps paradoxically, the major source that organizations have been able to count on to finance their advocacy and citizen engagement activity has been government, and study after study confirms a positive relationship between receipt of public funding and policy engagement. On the other hand, foundation funding seems to constrain advocacy activity, perhaps as a result of the restrictions on foundation support of lobbying written into the 1969 tax act.

In short, while the advocacy fire still burns within the nonprofit sector, it simmers at a relatively low temperature. What is more, it is increasingly selective in its focus. The public interest groups that made such a powerful political impact during the 1970s and 1980s differ markedly in their focus from the traditional working-class-oriented liberal and labor groups of the 1930s to 1950s. The political scientist Jeffrey Berry characterizes this as a shift from "materialism" to "postmaterialism," from the pocketbook concerns of middle- and working-class voters to the social concerns of more affluent ones.[63] The political awakening of the Christian Right has had a similar result, as Jacob Hacker and Paul Pierson observe in their powerful book, *Winner-Take-All Politics*. "Like the public interest groups on the left," Hacker and Pierson note, "the Christian Right has engaged voters on nonmaterial grounds. Moral values issues like abortion and gay marriage are the focus. And this concentration on moral issues has had a paradoxical consequence: It has aligned a large bloc of evangelical voters whose incomes are generally modest with a political party attuned to the economic demands of the wealthy. . . ."[64] Coupled with the emasculation of private sector unions, the result has been to open a significant vacuum with regard to advocacy and lobby support for issues relating to the poor and to the economic security of working-class people.

At the same time, business interests responded to the liberal environmental, consumer, and workplace safety victories of the 1960s and 1970s with a concerted organizational counterattack shepherded by a reinvigorated U.S. Chamber of Commerce and newly formed Business Roundtable. By 1982, 2,500 firms had registered lobbyists in Washington, up from 175 in 1971. The number of corporate PACs quadrupled between 1976 and 1980, and money poured into them. Despite efforts to impose legal limits on corporate and union campaign contributions, between the late 1970s and the late 1980s, corporate PAC contributions in congressional elections swelled by 500 percent, easily outdistancing labor contributions, even to Democratic candidates.[65] And this was before the landmark Supreme Court decision in *Citizens United* v. *Federal Election Commission* (2010), which freed corporations from any restrictions on their support of political candidates. And if labor has been outgunned as a consequence, so have public-interest advocacy and plain-vanilla non-profit service organizations, held back not only by legal and administrative limits on their involvement in policy activity, but also by limited resources of time and money. Under the circumstances, the prospects for a level playing field for nonprofits in the political arena seem increasingly remote, even given the advantages afforded by the new communications technologies and Internet-promoted demonstrations of the sort embodied in the Occupy Wall Street movement of 2011.

Summary and Implications

Nonprofit America has thus responded with extraordinary creativity and resilience to the challenges and opportunities it has confronted over the past thirty or so years. The sector has grown enormously as a consequence—in revenues, number of organizations, and the range of purposes it serves. In addition, the competencies and management of the sector's organizations have improved, though these are more difficult to gauge. To be sure, not all components of the sector have experienced these changes to the same degree or even in the same direction. Yet what is striking is how widespread the adaptations seem to have been.

In large part, what allowed nonprofit organizations not only to survive but to thrive during this period was that they moved, often decisively, toward the market. In the terms introduced earlier, the commercial impulse clearly gained the upper hand in nonprofit operations across a broad front. This did not mean, of course, that the other impulses pressing on the sector ceased to operate. To the contrary, nonprofits continued to promote advocacy and citizen engagement, though with somewhat subdued firepower; the voluntary impulse remained alive and well in the sector's public persona and in its attraction of charitable resources, volunteer effort, and new public programs supporting community service and faith-based organizations, even as the sector's center of gravity moved in a different direction; and professionalism continued to influence the sector's organizations, though more in their management than in the substance of their programs, thus moving nonprofit organizations ever closer to their for-profit cousins rather than their public-sector next of kin.

In short, while these other impulses continued to be felt, the commercial one seemed to gain the ascendance. Nonprofit organizations thus took advantage of the growing demand for their services, expanded their fee income, launched commercial ventures, forged partnerships with businesses, adopted business management techniques, mastered new consumer-side forms of government funding, reshaped their organizational structures, incorporated sophisticated marketing and money management techniques into even their charitable fundraising, and generally found new ways to tap the dynamism and resources of the market to promote their organizational objectives. This move toward the market has by no means been universal. Nor is it entirely new. What is more, it did not exhaust the range of responses the sector made to the challenges it faced. Yet it has clearly been the dominant theme of the past several decades, and its scope and impact have been profound, affecting all parts of the sector to some extent. As a result, the nonprofit sector is no longer your father's nonprofit sector. Rather, it has been substantially reengineered, and this process is still very much under way, though it has yet to be fully appreciated by the sector itself or by the nation at large.

The question for the future is what implications flow from this development for the viability and role of this important sector, and what, if anything, must be done to ensure that this sector not only survives, but also retains its distinctive place in national and community life. It is to this question that we turn next.

7

The Risks

As the previous chapters have indicated, the past thirty years or so have been a period of maturation and growth on the part of America's nonprofit sector. To an important degree, moreover, the sector has prospered by adopting many of the trappings and operations of the dominant market system. On balance, the resulting changes seem to have worked to the advantage of the nonprofit sector, strengthening its fiscal base, upgrading its operations, enlisting new partners and new resources in its activities, and generally improving its image for organizational effectiveness. But they have also brought significant risks, and the risks may well overwhelm the gains. Before drawing up the final balance sheet on the state of nonprofit America or its likely future evolution, therefore, it is necessary to weigh the gains against these risks and then consider what future steps may be needed.

More specifically, the nonprofit sector's response to the challenges of the past thirty years, creative as it has been, has exposed the sector to at least five new problems: a growing identity crisis, increased managerial demands, mission creep, disadvantaging of small agencies, and a loss of public trust. Let us examine each of these in turn.

Growing Identity Crisis

In the first place, the nonprofit sector is increasingly confronting an identity crisis as a result of a growing tension between the market character of the services it is providing and the continued nonprofit character of the institutions providing them. This tension has become especially stark in the health field, where third-party payers, such as Medicare and private HMOs, refuse to consider values other than actual service cost in setting reimbursement rates, and where bond-rating agencies discount community service in determining what nonprofit hospitals have to pay for the capital they need in order to expand.[1] Left to their own devices, nonprofit institutions have had little choice but to adjust to these pressures, but this adjustment comes at some cost to the features that make the institutions distinctive.

Under these circumstances, it is no wonder that scholars have been finding it difficult to detect real differences between the performance of for-profit and nonprofit hospitals and why many nonprofit HMOs and hospitals have surrendered the nonprofit form or sold out to for-profit firms.[2] Private universities are similarly experiencing strains between their mission to propagate knowledge and the expansion of their reliance on corporate sponsorship, which has brought with it demands for exclusive patent rights to the fruits of university research.[3] Marketing pressures are also intruding upon nonprofit arts and cultural institutions, limiting their ability to focus on artistic quality and transforming them into social enterprises focusing on market demands. So intense has the resulting identity crisis become, in fact, that some scholars are beginning to question the long-standing belief that nonprofits are reluctant participants in the market, providing only those "private goods" needed to support their "collective goods" activities, and are coming to see many nonprofits functioning instead as out-and-out commercial operations dominated by "pecuniary rather than altruistic objectives."[4]

Increased Demands on Nonprofit Managers

These tensions have naturally complicated the job of the nonprofit executive, requiring these officials to master not only the substantive dimensions of their fields but also the broader private markets within which they operate, the numerous public policies that affect them, and the massive new developments in technology and management with which they must contend. Nonprofit executives must do all this, moreover, while balancing a complex array of stakeholders that includes not only clients, staff, board members, and private donors but also regulators, government program officials, for-profit competitors, and business partners; and while also demonstrating performance and competing with other nonprofits and with for-profit firms for fees, board members, customers, contracts, grants, donations, gifts, bequests, visibility, prestige, political influence, and volunteers.[5] No wonder burnout has become such a serious problem in the field despite the excitement and fulfillment the role entails.

The Threat of Mission Creep

Inevitably, these pressures pose threats to the continued pursuit of nonprofit missions. Nonprofit organizations forced to rely on fees and charges naturally begin to skew their service offerings to clientele that are able to pay. What start out as sliding-fee scales designed to cross-subsidize services for the needy become core revenue sources essential for agency survival. Organizations needing to raise capital to expand are naturally tempted to locate new facilities in places with a client base able to finance the borrowing costs. When charity care, advocacy, and research are not covered in government or private reimbursement rates, institutions have little choice but to curtail these activities. Similarly, when new "impact investors" interested in measurable results for specific beneficiaries hold the upper hand in agency survival, hard-to-measure activities like advocacy and community organization may cease to seem important.[6]

How far these pressures have proceeded is difficult to say. Support for the poor has never been the exclusive, or the primary, focus of nonprofit action.[7] Nor need it be. What is more, many of the developments identified above have usefully mobilized market resources to support genuinely charitable purposes. Yet the nonprofit sector's movement toward the market is creating significant pressures to move away from those in greatest need, to focus on amenities that appeal to those who can pay, and to apply the market test to all facets of their operations.[8] The influence of the market impulse may thus be working at cross-purposes with the impulses to promote social justice and serve the poor—the impulses that government support, with all its limitations, opened up for significantly broader segments of the nonprofit sector in the post–World War II period.

Disadvantaging Small Agencies

A fourth risk resulting from the nonprofit sector's recent move to the market has been to put smaller agencies at an increasing disadvantage. Successful adaptation to the prevailing market pressures requires access to advanced technology, professional marketing, corporate partners, sophisticated fundraising, and complex government reimbursement systems, all of which are problematic for smaller agencies. Market pressures therefore create not simply a digital divide but a much broader "sustainability chasm," one that smaller organizations find difficult to bridge. Although some small agencies can cope with these pressures through collaborations and partnerships, these devices themselves often require sophisticated management; further, they absorb precious managerial energies.[9] As the barriers to entry, and particularly to sustainability, rise, the nonprofit sector is thus at risk of losing one of its most precious qualities— its ease of entry and its availability as a testing ground for new ideas.

Loss of Public Trust

All of this, finally, poses a further threat to the public trust on which the nonprofit sector ultimately depends. Thanks to the pressures they are under and the agility they have shown in response to them, American nonprofit organizations have moved well beyond the quaint Norman Rockwell stereotype of selfless volunteers ministering to the needy and supported largely by charitable gifts. Yet general public and media images remain wedded to this older stereotype and far too little attention has been given to bringing popular perceptions into better alignment with the realities that now exist, and to justifying these realities to a skeptical citizenry and press. As a consequence, nonprofits find themselves vulnerable when highly visible events, let alone instances of mismanagement or scandal, reveal them to be far more complex and commercially engaged institutions than the public suspects. The more successfully nonprofit organizations respond to the dominant market pressures, therefore, the greater risk they face of sacrificing the public trust on which they ultimately depend. This may help explain the widespread appeal of the Bush administration's "faith-based charities" initiative. What made this concept so appealing was its comforting affirmation of the older image of the nonprofit sector, the image of voluntary church groups staffed by the faithful solving the nation's problems of poverty and blight, even though this image grossly exaggerates both the capacity and the inclination of most congregations to engage in meaningful social problem solving.[10]

8

*The Road Ahead:
Toward a Renewal Strategy
for Nonprofit America*

As the introduction to this volume suggested, a struggle is under way for the "soul" of nonprofit America. In the terms introduced there, the sector and its individual organizations are caught in a force field among four competing pressures pulling them in a number of competing directions—toward voluntarism, professionalism, civic activism, and commercialism.

From the discussion above, it seems fair to conclude that the commercial and professional impulses may be gaining the upper hand and significantly displacing the voluntaristic and civic activist ones. This is important because it has implications for the balance that is struck between two crucial imperatives that this sector faces: a "distinctiveness imperative" challenging this sector to pay attention to the things that make nonprofits special and therefore justify the special tax and other privileges they enjoy, and a "survival imperative" challenging the sector to pay primary attention instead to the things it must do to survive.[1]

To be sure, these two imperatives are not wholly in conflict. Nevertheless, the tensions between them are real, and there is reason to worry that the survival imperative may have gained the upper hand. Left to their own devices in a demanding competitive environment, nonprofit leaders have understandably had to give survival precedence, and they have done so brilliantly, achieving a remarkable record of growth, adaptation, and resilience. What the discussion here suggests, however, is that this brilliant response has exposed the sector to potentially existential risks manifested, among other things, in new assaults on the charitable giving deduction, deepening exposure to local taxes and user fees, government payment methods that advantage for-profit vendors, and declining public understanding of how the sector operates, or why it is needed. As a consequence, it may be time to reset this balance.

Whether this will be possible will likely depend to a considerable extent on forces outside the sector's control—the shifting realities of political life, the resulting patterns of government policy, and broader economic, demographic, and technological trends. Nevertheless, sector leaders also have important choices.

Three Scenarios

Broadly speaking, at least three scenarios seem possible.

Celebration and Drift: The Status Quo Scenario

In the first place, the nonprofit sector can continue its historic posture of self-celebration and drift, emphasizing the virtues of charitable giving and volunteering, while drifting toward ever-greater reliance on commercial, or quasi-commercial, sources of support. Given the obvious strength of nonprofit organizations in a number of spheres, the reliance placed upon them by governments in crucial policy arenas, and the growing capability of nonprofit managers to balance the competing pressures they are facing, it seems likely that this scenario could sustain the sector for some time to come.

However, it is equally likely that a policy of drift will cause nonprofits to lose more of their market share, surrender more of their mission-critical functions such as advocacy and community organizing, and see the rai-son d'être for many of their special advantages, such as tax exemption, slip further away.

The Social Enterprise Scenario

A second scenario, especially attractive to younger activists and the so-cially conscious entrepreneurs from the dot.com industry, is to give up on the traditional nonprofit sector as it now exists and work toward the creation of a self-consciously new "social enterprise," or "fourth sector," one that explicitly merges social purpose with business methods and taps into the much larger resources available through socially focused private investment capital.

Hundreds of such social enterprises have surfaced in recent years both in the United States and around the world. Supporting this new wave of social-purpose businesses are capacity-builders like New Profit and Com-munity Wealth Ventures, enterprise brokers, as well as a growing num-ber of investment funds and investment vehicles.[2] Already, one portion of this fourth sector, composed of microenterprises and the "microfinance institutions" that support them, is estimated to have generated between $75 billion and $150 billion in investments, with prospects of growing into a much broader "microfinancial services" industry on a global scale.[3] Another branch is incubating a host of so-called bottom-of-the-pyramid businesses. These are businesses that design products and distribution channels that fit the economic resources of the millions of people at the bottom of the economic pyramid.[4] In the minds of many, these types of entities hold far more promise for solving the world's social and environ-mental problems than do traditional nonprofit organizations.

The Renewal Scenario

A third possible path of nonprofit evolution might be characterized as the "renewal option," and it is the option that this author favors. The key to this approach is to see the challenges facing the nonprofit sector not as an excuse for retreat into some pretended golden age of nonprofit independence, or as a time for continued drift toward greater commercialization, but rather as an opportunity for renewal, for rethinking the nonprofit sector's role and operations in light of contemporary realities, and for achieving a new consensus regarding the functions of these organizations, the relationships they have with citizens, with government, and with business, and the way they will operate in the years ahead.

The Renewal Strategy: A Deeper Dive

But what might such a renewal strategy for nonprofit America entail? Fundamentally, four processes of change seem most crucial.

Renewing the Nonprofit Value Proposition

At the center of the renewal scenario must be a clarification of the non-profit sector's "value proposition," the distinctive qualities and attributes nonprofit organizations bring to American society.[5] The voluntaristic impulse, after all, is not just about charitable giving and volunteer effort. This impulse is the carrier of a broader set of values that define the nonprofit sector's distinctive contributions—values of equity, openness, empowerment, participation, responsiveness, and commitment to the enrichment of human life. Thanks in part to the ascendance of the commercial impulse and its accompanying emphasis on metrics, however, many of these other values have been downplayed, and the value of the nonprofit sector reduced to the sector's service functions. While these functions are important, they hardly exhaust the value that Americans derive from nonprofit institutions. Clarifying these contributions and articulating them forcefully both for the sector as a whole and for particular organizations will be pivotal to the sector's ability to retain its special place in American life.

One recent attempt to do this was carried out by the consortium of organizations assembled under the banner of the Johns Hopkins Center for Civil Society Studies' Nonprofit Listening Post Project.[6] Working over several months, the steering committee of this project, made up of leaders

Box 8-1.   *The Nonprofit Value Proposition*

1) EFFECTIVE
- ✓ Providing programs and services of the highest quality at reasonable cost
- ✓ Making a difference in the lives of individuals and the community

2) RESPONSIVE
- ✓ Responding to clients, patrons, and communities
- ✓ Meeting needs that the market and government don't meet
- ✓ Pursuing innovative approaches when needed

3) RELIABLE
- ✓ Demonstrating staying power in both good times and bad
- ✓ Operating in a trustworthy and accountable manner

4) CARING
- ✓ Serving underserved populations
- ✓ Providing services/programs at reduced or no cost to disadvantaged populations
- ✓ Focusing on communities

5) ENRICHING
- ✓ Giving expression to central human values
- ✓ Providing opportunities for people to learn and grow
- ✓ Fostering intellectual, scientific, cultural, and spiritual development
- ✓ Preserving culture and history; promoting creativity

6) EMPOWERING
- ✓ Mobilizing and empowering citizens
- ✓ Contributing to public discourse
- ✓ Providing opportunities for civic engagement

7) PRODUCTIVE
- ✓ Creating jobs and economic value
- ✓ Mobilizing assets to address public problems
- ✓ Enhancing local economic vitality

Source: See chapter 8, note 8.

of eleven leading nonprofit intermediary organizations in the fields of elderly services, family and children's services, disability, community development, and the arts, identified a series of seven attributes that seemed to form the core of the nonprofit sector's value proposition.[7] As reflected in box 8-1, these attributes emphasize the aspiration of this sector to be considered *effective, responsive, reliable, caring, enriching, empowering,* and *productive,* the latter in the sense of creating jobs and economic value.

A survey was then distributed to 1,500 nonprofit organizations in the fields of social services, community development, and the arts in late 2011 and early 2012 to determine whether these attributes captured the core value add of this sector in the minds of its practitioners and to assess how well they thought the sector was both embodying and articulating these values. The results of this survey were revealing. (For illustrations of how respondents understood these various attributes, see boxes 8-2 through 8-5.)[8]

In the first place, despite their diversity, the respondents were overwhelmingly in agreement that these seven attributes describe this sector's core values, as shown in figure 8-1. At the same time, there were some potentially significant variations. For instance, while 79 or more percent of respondents rated each of the three top values—being *effective, responsive,* and *reliable*—as "very important," only 56 percent gave the same rating to being *empowering.* This is surprising because civic advocacy has long been considered a critical function of the nonprofit sector. This finding thus adds credence to the concern that fiscal pressures on nonprofits, limitations on financial support for advocacy, and the drive toward more readily measurable service functions as part of a shift toward commercialism may be muting this function.

An even smaller 52 percent of respondents rated being *productive* as "very important." This may simply reflect the fact that many nonprofits do not think of themselves in terms of their economic function. But given the current emphasis on jobs and economic recovery, this may be an important misperception to correct as part of any renewal strategy—especially since existing data show that nonprofits do, in fact, have substantial economic impact, as previous chapters have shown.

Figure 8-1. *Extent of Nonprofit Agreement on Core Values of the Sector (Weighted Average)*

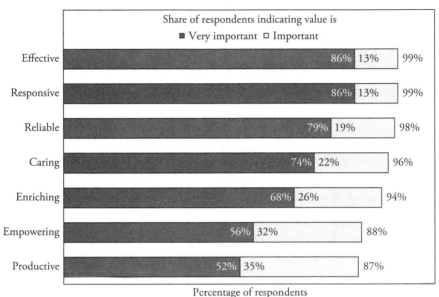

Source: Salamon, Geller, and Newhouse, "What Do Nonprofits Stand For?"

A second key finding was that respondents were overwhelmingly of the opinion that they embodied these core values "well," or "very well," though the proportions claiming to do so "very well" did not exceed 72 percent for any of the values. And when it came to the values of being *empowering* and *productive,* the proportions claiming to be performing "very well" fell to 31 and 25 percent, respectively. Even among community development groups, the organizations with the greatest connection to disadvantaged communities, and the group with the highest proportion reporting satisfaction with the extent to which they embody the *empowerment* attribute, only 39 percent claimed to be doing "very well" in delivering on this value. Similarly, even among the largest organizations, those with annual revenues in excess of $3 million, only a third reported doing "very well" in embodying the value of being *productive* contributors to their local economies. These findings are all the more significant in view of the fact that the quality of being *empowering* is one of three

---

Box 8-2. *Being "Effective"*

"Over 75 years, our programs have demonstrated their effectiveness at helping young people achieve economic self-sufficiency in
adulthood. This comes from tracking graduates in the last
35 years. We have data on more than 2/3 of the group and more
than 94% no longer live in poverty."

*A midsize children and family services
organization on being EFFECTIVE*

Source: Salamon, Geller, and Newhouse, "What Do Nonprofits Stand For?"

in which nonprofits are in general agreement that they outdistance the
for-profit sector (the other two are being *caring* and *enriching*).

While acknowledging lapses in their own embodiment of these various values, over half of these nonprofit respondents expressed the belief
that the general public and government officials have little grasp of the
nonprofit sector's special qualities, and over 60 percent acknowledged that
the nonprofit sector itself may be at fault by not articulating the sector's
value proposition sufficiently to those outside the sector. Respondents
were overwhelmingly convinced that remedying this shortcoming is a
high-priority task for the sector, that without it the sector is in significant danger, but that help is needed to determine how best this can be
done. In short, there was significant endorsement of a renewal effort, and a
renewal effort built around a values framework of the sort described here.

Improving the Government-Nonprofit Partnership

Equally important to the renewal scenario is the acknowledgment, indeed celebration, of the nonprofit sector's role as government's "partner
in public service."[9] The sector's role as the delivery system for publicly
funded services that expand opportunities and improve the quality of life
for millions of citizens needs to be made more explicit. As noted, government has emerged as the second most important source of nonprofit
revenue in the United States, outdistancing philanthropy by a factor of

---

Box 8-3.　*Being "Productive"*

"We built our new facility in an economically depressed area of the community because it is where many of the people we serve are living. It was a $3 million investment in an area that for-profits haven't invested in, and brought 50 employees and activity to a neighborhood sorely in need of it."

A large children and family services
organization on being PRODUCTIVE

Source: Salamon, Geller, and Newhouse, "What Do Nonprofits Stand For?"

nearly four to one. And in Western Europe that role is even greater. Yet the nonprofit sector's relationship with government in the United States remains suspect in the minds of many and poorly understood among most of the rest. At the same time, this relationship, for all its strengths, remains in need of restructuring and reconstruction. As a declaration by leaders representing over 100,000 nonprofit organizations noted recently, "The relationships between government and the nonprofit sector have evolved in ad hoc fashion, with too little attention to their operational inefficiencies or to their tendency to put valued characteristics of the citizen-sector at risk."[10]

Other countries have dealt with these problems by forging compacts between government and nonprofit organizations in order to make their collaborations operate better for both sides. While such overarching policy prescriptions are difficult to establish in America's fragmented political system, more explicit recognition is needed that this partnership offers enormous advantages to government, to nonprofits, and to the citizens they both serve, but that significant improvements are needed to allow it to achieve its promise more effectively. Such recognition would begin by acknowledging government's stake in the nonprofit delivery system for government programs and the resulting need for governmental investment in the capacity of its nonprofit partners.

Equally important is explicit acknowledgment in government grants, contracts, and reimbursement systems of the need to protect

---

Box 8-4.   *Being "Reliable" and "Enriching"*

"During a weather emergency that had government agencies and roads closed for several days, our volunteer corps walked to make wellness checks and deliver meals to our frail elderly clients."

*A large elderly housing and services
organization on being RELIABLE*

"2,048 schoolchildren who visit on field trips would not otherwise be challenged or experience art, history, and science in this rural community in a context relevant to them."

A midsize museum on being ENRICHING

Source: Salamon, Geller, and Newhouse, "What Do Nonprofits Stand For?"

the mission-critical functions of nonprofits, such as advocacy and community organizing, so that nonprofits can continue to perform their important empowerment functions. Whether nonprofit hospitals can continue to support their teaching and research functions, for example, is significantly affected by whether Medicare considers this function vital enough to be covered in the reimbursement rates for nonprofit hospitals. But rather than protecting and encouraging these important nonprofit functions, government policy in recent years has moved in the direction of constraining them, especially in the advocacy arena. In the prevailing deregulation climate, some significant deregulation of nonprofit advocacy and lobbying also therefore seems in order.

Beyond this, government needs to commit to full coverage of the costs of the services it depends on nonprofits to deliver, and timely payment on grants and contracts. In the process, nonprofits will need to accept the legitimate accountability requirements of government.

Strengthening Nonprofit Finance

Any serious renewal scenario must also address the perennial problems of nonprofit finance, and particularly the problem of nonprofit access to

---

Box 8-5.   *Being "Responsive"*

"After Katrina, when there were no other social service agencies in our community, we rapidly shifted to meet the needs of the community and adapted our methods, techniques and foci as the needs changed and time progressed. Government and the for-profit sector lacked this social entrepreneurism and were late to the game."

A small community and economic development
organization on being RESPONSIVE

Source: Salamon, Geller, and Newhouse, "What Do Nonprofits Stand For?"

investment capital. As we have seen, nonprofits confront an uneven playing field in this area due to their lack of access to the equity markets. As a consequence, they have frequently lost market share even in fields that they pioneered. Significant developments on the frontiers of philanthropy hold promise for improving nonprofit access to investment capital, but these could benefit greatly from government encouragement.

The experience of nonprofit hospitals, higher education institutions, and low-income housing organizations is instructive in this regard. The experience of the first two demonstrates that nonprofit organizations can often hold their own in the face of stiff for-profit competition when they can gain access to needed capital at competitive rates. In both of these cases, special tax incentives have been available to subsidize bonds issued to finance nonprofit facilities. The example of the nonprofit housing organizations mentioned earlier demonstrates that the same approach can be successfully used for organizations serving disadvantaged groups. Here, passage of the Low-Income Housing Tax Credit program, coupled with the emergence of nonprofit intermediary institutions that package the resulting tax breaks for sale to investors, has opened a significant flow of private investment capital into low-income housing.[11] Broadening this tax credit to cover investments in other nonprofit facilities or equipment serving disadvantaged persons would go a long way toward keeping nonprofits competitive in a wider range of fields.

Other steps could include broadening the coverage of the Community Reinvestment Act to apply to insurance companies and other financial service firms to add a regulatory nudge to the maturation of the social-impact investing field. As I have written elsewhere, this field is "still a boutique business" that needs a push to take off.[12] Another useful step would be clarification of the "prudent person rules" for foundation investment in social-impact investing. Many foundations have evolved into veritable "philanthropic banks," utilizing their assets and not just their grant budgets to support their programmatic missions, but others hold back because of fears that regulators will accuse them of failing in their fiduciary "duty of care."[13] Similarly, rigid features of the laws governing pension funds have the same effect, constraining rather than encouraging participation in a form of investment that has proved to be quite solid and at least as reliable as many mainline investments.[14]

Also needed—given the likely near-term constraints on government funding—is some way to stimulate greater charitable giving. The recent expansion of web-based giving seems likely to help in this, though experience suggests that such giving is episodic and crisis related. Another approach might be to move toward a system of tax credits instead of tax deductions. Unlike deductions, which deliver more tax benefits per dollar contributed to persons in high tax brackets than in low ones, tax credits provide the same tax benefits to all contributors regardless of their income.[15] In addition, tax credits can be made available to all contributors regardless of whether they itemize their tax deductions. Since 75 percent of taxpayers currently take the so-called standard deduction and therefore do not itemize, a shift to a tax credit system would further democratize giving.

The major obstacle to this approach is that it could provide a windfall benefit to people who would be making contributions anyway, but this could be remedied by setting a floor under the amount of gifts that would qualify for credits. American charitable giving has been stuck at 2 percent of personal income or less for some time. It is worth considering approaches that might boost this level in the future, and a system of tax credits instead of deductions might well be one worth trying.

Improving Public Understanding

Finally, any renewal scenario will require a major investment in public education. What is needed here, however, is not another celebration of private giving and volunteering, important though these are. Rather, the public must be introduced to the broader realities of current nonprofit operations, to the impressive resilience that the sector exhibits, and to the special qualities that make nonprofit organizations worth protecting. Also required is a better public defense of the sector's long-standing partnership with government and a clarification of the crucial role nonprofits play as key links working collaboratively with government and the business sector to solve public problems. This may be a complex message to convey, but it is the one that best reflects the current realities and perhaps the best hope for the nonprofit sector's future.

Conclusion

It has been said that the quality of a nation can be seen in the way it treats its least advantaged citizens. But it can also be seen in the way it treats its most valued institutions. Americans have long paid lip service to the importance they attach to their voluntary institutions, while largely ignoring the challenges these institutions face. During the past two decades, these challenges have been extraordinary. But so too has been the nonprofit sector's response. As a result, the state of nonprofit America is surprisingly robust as we approach the third decade of the new millennium, with more organizations doing more things more effectively than ever before.

At the same time, the movement to the market that has made this possible has also exposed the sector to enormous risks, endangering its future evolution and its hold on the public's trust. What is more, the risks go to the heart of what makes the nonprofit sector distinctive and worthy of public support—its basic identity, its underlying values, its mission, and its ability to retain public support.

Up to now, nonprofit managers have had to fend for themselves in deciding what risks it was acceptable to take in order to permit their organizations to survive. Given the stake that American society has in the preservation of these institutions and in the protection of their ability to perform their distinctive roles, it seems clear that this must now change. Americans need to rethink whether the balance that has been struck among the four impulses driving the nonprofit sector, and between the survival and distinctiveness imperatives that lie behind them, is the right one for the future—and if not, what steps might now be needed to shift this balance for the years ahead.

The argument here is that some such adjustments are needed, that America's nonprofit institutions require broader support in preserving the features that make them special. Whether others agree with this conclusion remains to be seen. What seems clear, however, is that better public understanding of the state of nonprofit America is needed if such judgments are to be possible. Hopefully, the analysis in this book will contribute to such understanding. That, at any rate, has been its goal.

Notes

Chapter 1

1. D. A. Whetten and P. C. Godfrey, *Identity in Organization* (London: Sage, 1998); Mary Ann Glynn, "When Cymbals Become Symbols: Conflict over Organizational Identity within a Symphony Orchestra," *Organizational Science* 11, no. 3 (2000), p. 285.

2. For a discussion of this partnership, see Lester M. Salamon, "Partners in Public Service," in *The Nonprofit Sector: A Research Handbook,* edited by Walter W. Powell (Yale University Press, 1987), pp. 99–117; and Lester M. Salamon, *Partners in Public Service: Government-Nonprofit Relations in the Modern Welfare State* (Johns Hopkins University Press, 1995).

3. Michael S. Joyce and William A. Schambra, "A New Civic Life," in *To Empower People: From State to Civil Society,* edited by Michael Novak, 2nd ed. (Washington: AEI Press, 1996), pp. 11–29; Robert Nisbet, *Community and Power,* 2nd ed. (Oxford University Press, 1962).

4. Carmen Sirianni and Lewis Friedland, *Civic Innovation in America: Community Empowerment, Public Policy, and the Movement for Civic Renewal* (University of California Press, 2001); Harry Boyte, *Commonwealth: A Return to Citizen Politics* (Galway: MW Books, 1989); John McKnight, *The Careless Society: Community and Its Counterfeit* (New York: Basic Books, 1995).

5. Alexis de Tocqueville, *Democracy in America,* vol. 2, trans. Henry Reeve, rev. Francis Bowen (1835; reprint, New York: Vintage Books, 1945), p. 118.

6. For the full results of this larger project, see Lester M. Salamon, ed., *The State of Nonprofit America,* 2nd ed. (Brookings, 2012). The present book originally appeared in somewhat abridged form as chapter 1 of this broader volume, though it has been updated here.

7. On the reengineering movement in the corporate sector, see Michael Hammer and James Champy, *Reengineering the Corporation: A Manifesto for Business Revolution* (London: Nicholas Brealey, 1994); David K. Carr and Henry J. Johnson, *Best Practices in Reengineering: What Works and What Doesn't in the Reengineering Process* (New York: McGraw-Hill, 1995).

8. I am indebted to Bradford Gray and Mark Schlesinger for introducing this concept. See Bradford H. Gray and Mark Schlesinger, "Health Care," in *The State of Nonprofit America,* edited by Salamon, pp. 123–25.

Chapter 2

1. Federal tax law identifies at least twenty-six classes of such organizations, ranging from political parties to cemetery companies. Nonprofits are required to pay taxes on any so-called unrelated business profits they may earn. For a fuller discussion of the legal definition of a tax-exempt or nonprofit organization, see Bruce R. Hopkins, *The Law of Tax-Exempt Organizations,* 9th ed. (New York: Wiley, 2007), pp. 3–23. See also Lester M. Salamon, *America's Nonprofit Sector: A Primer,* 3rd ed. (New York: Foundation Center, 2012).

2. This difference between 501(c)(3) and 501(c)(4) organizations with respect to lobbying activity is notoriously unclear. The difference hinges on the definition of lobbying as opposed to advocacy, and that definition is rather complex. Advocacy refers to any effort to inform policymakers or the public about public problems and possible government or private actions that might be needed to resolve them. Lobbying is a narrower concept and refers to specific attempts to influence the passage or defeat of particular laws, either directly, by influencing legislators, or indirectly, by mobilizing broader public efforts to influence legislators. Both 501(c)(3) and 501(c)(4) organizations are free to engage in advocacy activities without limit, but 501(c)(3)s are only allowed to participate in lobbying activities to an "insubstantial" extent. What an insubstantial extent actually consists of has never been fully explicated in legislation or court interpretations, though recent legislation has given 501(c)(3) organizations the option of accepting a legislative schedule of permissible resources that can be devoted to such activity. For further detail, see Hopkins, *Law of Tax-Exempt Organizations,* pp. 400–04.

3. Although churches are actually member-serving organizations, we include them in the public-serving portion of the sector because they enjoy their tax-exempt status under section 501(c)(3) of the Internal Revenue Code. Alone among (c)(3) organizations, however, churches are not required to register with the Internal Revenue Service or to file the Form 990 required of all other (c)(3) organizations, but some churches do file. The estimate of just over 1.7 million identifiable nonprofit organizations noted here was derived by adding our best estimate of the number of churches not included on the Exempt Organization Master File (EOMF) records to the 1,533,853 nonprofit organizations identified on the recently revised IRS EOMF. The IRS EOMF data were derived from IRS data files: Internal Revenue Service, "Exempt Organizations Business Master File Extract (EO BMF)" (www .irs.gov/Charities-&-Non-Profits/Exempt-Organizations-Business-Master-File -Extract-EO-BMF) [accessed on February 10, 2015]. The estimate of the number of religious congregations was compiled from several sources. These included Eileen Lindner, ed., *Yearbook of American and Canadian Churches, 2010,* prepared for the National Council of the Churches of Christ (Nashville: Abingdon Press, 2010); the Association of Religion Data Archives, "U.S. Membership Report, 2000" (www .thearda.com/mapsReports/reports/US_2000.asp); and Mark Chaves, "Religious Congregations," in *The State of Nonprofit America,* edited by Lester M. Salamon, 2nd ed. (Brookings, 2012), pp. 362–93. Altogether, this yielded an estimate of 428,975 congregations. Since 220,293 churches were found on the revised and updated EOMF records as of 2014, this meant the addition of 208,000 churches to the organizations recorded on the EOMF. For further details on these sources, see Salamon, *America's Nonprofit Sector,* p. 58, n. 2.

4. These figures come from Quarterly Census of Employment and Wages (QCEW) data published online by the U.S. Bureau of Labor Statistics (BLS) (www .bls.gov/data/). The nonprofit figures include all 501(c)(3) organizations identified in QCEW. Volunteering data were tabulated from the September Supplement to the *Current Population Survey* available online through DataFerret (http://data ferrett.census.gov/).

5. The estimates reported here, in the subsequent paragraph, and in figure 2-2, cover only organizations that filed a Form 990 or 990PF and were computed chiefly from Internal Revenue Service Statistics of Income microdata estimates compiled from a sample of Form 990 and Form 990EZ forms submitted by U.S. nonprofit organizations and then blown up to represent the population of such filers. The data were extracted from the Statistics of Income (SOI) website: Internal Revenue Service, "SOI Tax Stats—Charities and Other Tax-Exempt Organizations Statistics" (www.irs.gov/uac/SOI-Tax-Stats-Charities-and-Other-Tax-Exempt -Organizations-Statistics). This source was supplemented by estimates developed by the Bureau of Economic Analysis (BEA) on the revenues of religious organizations whose income is not recorded by the IRS since religious organizations

are not required to file Form 990. The BEA data were found in NIPA table 7.19 at (www.bea.gov/iTable/iTable.cfm?ReqID=9&step=1#reqid=9&step=3&isuri =1&903=297).

6. Kennard T. Wing, Thomas H. Pollack, and Amy Blackwood, *The Nonprofit Almanac, 2008* (Washington: Urban Institute, 2008), pp. 228–35.

7. Based on Internal Revenue Service EOMF and SOI data. See notes 3 and 5, respectively, above.

8. Wing, Pollack, and Blackwood, *Nonprofit Almanac, 2008,* p. 142.

9. The data reported here draw primarily on microdata files prepared by the Internal Revenue Service from Form 990 filings required of all nonprofit organizations with $25,000 or more of annual income. Foundations and other funding intermediaries, as well as religious congregations, were removed from the data to avoid double counting of contributions and to zero in on the service and expressive organizations of principal concern to us. The microdata files were accessed at the Internal Revenue Service "SOI Tax Stats" identified in note 5 above. Because Form 990 lumps together as "program service revenue" government contract payments, government voucher payments such as Medicare and Medicaid, and direct purchases paid for by consumers, the published data obscure the true extent of government support flowing to nonprofit organizations. Since these government "purchases" are huge, it was necessary to disentangle this "program service revenue" category and provide a clearer picture of the totality of direct government support to nonprofit service and expressive organizations. This was done by using the nonprofit share of total employment in health (NAICS Codes 621 and 622) as a proxy for the nonprofit share of Medicare and Medicaid payments and applying this against data secured from the BEA's National Income and Product Account table 3.12. For further detail on how this was done, see Salamon, *America's Nonprofit Sector,* chapter 3, n. 18.

10. See, for example, James S. Coleman, *Foundations of Social Theory* (Harvard University Press, 1990), pp. 300–21; Robert D. Putnam, *Making Democracy Work: Civic Traditions in Modern Italy* (Princeton University Press, 1993), pp. 83–116, 163–85.

11. Alexis de Tocqueville, *Democracy in America,* vol. 2, trans. Henry Reeve, rev. Francis Bowen (1835; reprint, New York: Vintage Books, 1945), p. 117.

12. The term *value guardian* was first used by Ralph Kramer, *Voluntary Agencies in the Welfare State* (University of California Press, 1981), pp. 193–211, to describe one of the crucial roles of nonprofit organizations. Kramer refers mostly to volunteering, but it has a broader meaning as well.

Chapter 3

1. Waldemar Nielsen, *The Endangered Sector* (Columbia University Press, 1979), pp. 24–25.

2. See, for example, Robert Nisbet, *Community and Power,* 2nd ed. (Oxford University Press, 1962); Peter D. Berger and Richard Neuhaus, *To Empower People: The Role of Mediating Structures in Public Policy* (Washington: AEI Press, 1977); Michael S. Joyce and William A. Schambra, "A New Civic Life," in *To Empower People: From State to Civil Society,* edited by Michael Novak, 2nd ed. (Washington: AEI Press, 1996), pp. 11–29; Leslie Lenkowsky, "Philanthropy and the Welfare State," in *To Empower People,* edited by Novak, pp. 90–91.

3. This portrait of the characteristics of the voluntaristic impulse draws on a variety of sources, including Stuart Langton, "The New Voluntarism," *Nonprofit and Voluntary Sector Quarterly* 10 (January 1981), pp. 7–20; Barry D. Karl, "Volunteers and Professionals: Many Histories, Many Meanings," in *Private Action and the Public Good,* edited by Walter W. Powell and Elizabeth Clemens (Yale University Press, 1998), pp. 248–57; Peter Frumkin, *On Being Nonprofit: A Conceptual and Policy Primer* (Harvard University Press, 2002); Joyce and Schambra, "New Civic Life"; Karin Kreutzer and Urs Jäger, "Volunteering versus Managerialism: Conflict over Organizational Identity in Voluntary Associations," *Nonprofit and Voluntary Sector Quarterly* 40, no. 4 (2011), pp. 634–61; Robert L. Woodson Sr., "Success Stories," in *To Empower People,* edited by Novak, pp. 105–15.

4. The usage of the term *professional* here thus corresponds to what Hwang and Powell refer to as "traditional ideal-type professionals" or "subject-matter professionals," as opposed to those whose expertise is in general management. See Hokyu Hwang and Walter W. Powell, "The Rationalization of Charity: The Influences of Professionalism in the Nonprofit Sector," *Administrative Science Quarterly* 54, no. 2 (2009), pp. 268–75. I refer to this latter as *managerial professionalism* as opposed to *professionalism.* On the definition of *subject-matter professionalism,* see also Karl, "Volunteers and Professionals," p. 246; Harold Wilensky, "The Professionalization of Everyone?," *American Journal of Sociology* 70, no. 2 (1964), pp. 137–58. For a definition of managerialism, see Kreutzer and Jäger, "Volunteering versus Managerialism."

5. See, for example, Judith A. Trolander, *Professionalism and Social Change: From the Settlement House Movement to Neighborhood Centers, 1886 to the Present* (Columbia University Press, 1987), pp. 39, 238–39; Roy Lubove, *The Professional Altruist: The Emergence of Social Work as a Career, 1880–1930* (Harvard University Press, 1965), pp. 49–53; David Rosner, *A Once Charitable Enterprise: Hospitals and Health Care in Brooklyn and New York, 1885–1915* (Cambridge University Press, 1982), pp. 6–12.

6. According to Harold Wilensky, there are at least five steps crucial to the establishment of a profession: full-time work, a curriculum and training schools, a

professional association, official licensing or certification requirements, and a formal code of ethics, Wilensky, "Professionalization of Everyone?," 142–46.

7. Rosner, *Once Charitable Enterprise*, p. 6.

8. Lubove, *Professional Altruist*, p. 48.

9. Trolander, *Professionalism and Social Change*, p. 40; Karl, "Volunteers and Professionals," p. 256.

10. Lubove, *Professional Altruist*, p. 23.

11. The portrayal of the civic activism impulse here draws on Vernon Jordan, "Voluntarism in America," *Vital Speeches* 43, no. 16 (1977), p. 493; Langton, "New Voluntarism," pp. 10–11; Theda Skocpol, *Diminished Democracy: From Membership to Management in American Civic Life* (Oklahoma University Press, 1987); Frumkin, *On Being Nonprofit*, pp. 29–31, 53–61; Carmen Sirianni and Lewis Friedland, *Civic Innovation in America: Community Empowerment, Public Policy, and the Movement for Civic Renewal* (University of California Press, 2001); Harry Boyte, *Commonwealth: A Return to Citizen Politics* (Galway: MW Books, 1989).

12. Trolander, *Professionalism and Social Change*, p. 1.

13. Brian O'Connell, "From Service to Advocacy to Empowerment," *Social Casework* 59 (April 1978), p. 198.

14. The description of the characteristics of the commercial impulse here draws on the following sources, among others: Hwang and Powell, "Rationalization of Charity"; Kreutzer and Jäger, "Volunteering versus Managerialism"; Frumkin, *On Being Nonprofit*, pp. 129–62; Lester M. Salamon, "The Marketization of Welfare: Changing Nonprofit and For-Profit Roles in the American Welfare State," *Social Service Review* 67, no. 1 (1993), pp. 17–39; Angela Eikenberry and Jodie Drapal Kluver, "The Marketization of the Nonprofit Sector: Civil Society at Risk?," *Public Administration Review* 64, no. 2 (2004), pp. 132–40; Howard P. Tuckman, "Competition, Commercialization, and the Evolution of Nonprofit Organizational Structures," in *To Profit or Not to Profit: The Commercial Transformation of the Nonprofit Sector,* edited by Burton A. Weisbrod (Cambridge University Press, 1998), pp. 25–46; Burton A. Weisbrod, "Modeling the Nonprofit Organization as a Multiproduct Firm: A Framework for Choice," in *To Profit or Not to Profit,* edited by Weisbrod, pp. 47–64; Kevin P. Kearns, *Private Sector Strategies for Social Sector Success: The Guide to Strategy and Planning for Public and Nonprofit Organizations* (San Francisco: Jossey-Bass, 2000).

Chapter 4

1. Stuart Langton, "The New Voluntarism," *Nonprofit and Voluntary Sector Quarterly* 10 (January 1981), p. 9.

2. See C. K. Prahalad, *The Fortune at the Bottom of the Pyramid: Eradicating Poverty through Profits,* rev. ed. (Philadelphia: Wharton School Publishing, 2010); Alex Nichols, ed., *Social Entrepreneurship: New Models of Sustainable Social Change* (Oxford University Press, 2006); David Bornstein, *How to Change the World: Social Entrepreneurs and the Power of New Ideas* (Oxford University Press, 2004).

3. The data here and in figure 4-1 are based on U.S. Bureau of Economic Analysis, *National Income and Product Accounts,* table 3.16 (www.bea.gov/iTable /iTable.cfm?ReqID=9&step=1#reqid=9&step=3&isuri=1&903=119). For our purposes here, government social welfare spending includes the following fields: health, education, income security (retirement, disability, unemployment insurance, welfare, and social services), and housing and community services.

4. For a more complete analysis of this system of government-nonprofit relations and the broader pattern of third-party government of which it is a part, see Lester M. Salamon, "Partners in Public Service," in *The Nonprofit Sector: A Research Handbook,* edited by Walter W. Powell (Yale University Press, 1987); and Lester M. Salamon, *Partners in Public Service: Government-Nonprofit Relations in the Modern Welfare State* (Johns Hopkins University Press, 1995). For a discussion of the federal government's support of nonprofit research universities, see Don K. Price, *The Scientific Estate* (Harvard University Press, 1965). For the early roots of government support of nonprofit organizations in the United States, see John S. Whitehead, *The Separation of College and State: Columbia, Dartmouth, Harvard, and Yale* (Yale University Press, 1973), pp. 3–16; Amos Warner, *American Charities: A Study in Philanthropy and Economics* (New York: Thomas Y. Crowell, 1894), pp. 400–05.

5. Lester M. Salamon and Alan J. Abramson, *The Federal Budget and the Nonprofit Sector* (Washington: Urban Institute, 1982).

6. Lester M. Salamon and Alan J. Abramson, "The Federal Budget and the Nonprofit Sector: Implications of the Contract with America," in *Capacity for Change? The Nonprofit World in the Age of Devolution,* edited by Dwight F. Burlingame et al. (Center on Philanthropy, Indiana University, 1996), pp. 8–9; Alan J. Abramson, Lester M. Salamon, and C. Eugene Steuerle, "The Nonprofit Sector and the Federal Budget: Recent History and Future Directions," in *Nonprofits and Government: Collaboration and Conflict,* edited by Elizabeth T. Boris and C. Eugene Steuerle (Washington: Urban Institute, 1999), pp. 110–12.

7. U.S. House of Representatives, Committee on Ways and Means, *2000 Green Book: Background Material and Data on Programs within the Jurisdiction of the Committee on Ways and Means,* 106th Cong., 2nd sess. (Government Printing Office, 2000), p. 214. As a consequence, the number of children covered by SSI increased from 71,000 in 1974 to over 1 million in 1996, boosting expenditures in real terms from $16.4 billion in 1980 to $30.2 billion in 1999.

8. Medicaid coverage was extended to fifty distinct subgroups during the late 1980s and early 1990s, including the homeless, newly legalized aliens, AIDS sufferers, recipients of adoption assistance and foster care, and broader categories of the disabled and the elderly. Between 1980 and 1998, as a consequence, Medicaid coverage jumped from 21.6 million to 40.6 million people. At the same time, the services these programs cover also expanded dramatically. Thus, skilled nursing care, home health care, hospice care, and kidney dialysis services became eligible for Medicare coverage. Intermediate care for the mentally retarded, home health care, family planning, clinic care, child welfare services, and rehabilitation services were added to Medicaid. These changes, coupled with state options to add additional services (such as physical therapy, medical social worker counseling, case management, and transportation), transformed Medicaid from a relatively narrow health and nursing home program into a social service entitlement program. Reflecting these changes, spending on the major federal entitlement programs jumped nearly 200 percent in real terms between 1980 and 1999, more than twice the 81 percent growth in GDP. House Committee on Ways and Means, *2000 Green Book*, pp. 924, 927.

9. Ibid., pp. 597, 953–54.

10. Mental health, mental retardation, maternal and child health rehabilitation, and AIDS services were special targets for this strategy, particularly as Medicaid expanded eligibility for pregnant women and children, and SSI (and hence Medicaid) expanded coverage for AIDS patients and the disabled. Teresa Coughlin, Leighton Ku, and John Holahan, *Medicaid since 1980* (Washington: Urban Institute, 1984), p. 87. For further detail, see Steve Smith, "Social Services," in *The State of Nonprofit America,* edited by Lester M. Salamon, 2nd ed. (Brookings, 2012), pp. 192–228.

11. The number of people on welfare fell by half between 1994 and 1999, from 14.2 million to 7.2 million. In addition, the portion of those remaining on the rolls requiring full cash grants also declined, because more of them were working. Since states were guaranteed federal grants under the new Temporary Assistance for Needy Families (TANF) program at their peak levels of the early 1990s, and were also obligated to maintain their own spending on needy families at 75 percent of their previous levels, funding for services increased. By 1999, for example, spending on direct cash assistance under the welfare program had fallen to 60 percent of the total funds available, leaving 40 percent for child care, work readiness, drug abuse treatment, and related purposes. House Committee on Ways and Means, *2000 Green Book,* pp. 376, 411.

12. Elizabeth Schwinn, "Bush's Budget Plan," *Chronicle of Philanthropy,* February 27, 2007 (http://philanthropy.com/article/Charities-Face-Challenges -From/126375/); Brennen Jensen and Suzanne Perry, "A Budget Squeeze Hits Charities: Bush's 2009 Plan Calls for Cuts in Social Services and the Arts,"

Chronicle of Philanthropy, February 21, 2008 (http://philanthropy.com/article/A
-Budget-Squeeze-Hits/61350/).

13. Robert Pear, "Obama Proposes $320 Billion in Medicare and Medicaid
Cuts over 10 Years," *New York Times,* September 20, 2011, p. A15 (www.nytimes
.com/2011/09/20/us/politics/medicare-and-medicaid-face-320-billion-in-cuts
-over-10-years.html); Jackie Calmes, "Obama Confirms New Hard Stand with
Debt Relief," *New York Times,* September 20, 2011, p. A1 (www.nytimes.com
/2011/09/20/us/politics/obama-vows-veto-if-deficit-plan-has-no-tax-increases
.html).

14. U.S. Office of Management and Budget, "Enhancing Governmental Productivity through Competition: A New Way of Doing Business within the Government to Provide Quality Government at Least Cost," cited in Donald Kettl,
Shared Power: Public Governance and Private Markets (Brookings, 1993), p. 46.

15. Vouchers essentially provide targeted assistance to eligible recipients in the
form of a certificate or a reimbursement card that can be presented to the provider
of choice. The provider then receives payment for the certificate or reimbursement
from the government. Tax expenditures use a similar method except that no
actual certificate is used. Rather, eligible taxpayers are allowed to deduct a given
proportion of the cost of a particular service (such as day care) either from their
income before computing their tax obligations (tax deduction) or directly from
the taxes they owe (tax credit). For a general discussion of these alternative tools of
public action, see Lester M. Salamon, "The New Governance and the Tools of
Public Action: An Introduction," in *The Tools of Government: A Guide to the New
Governance,* edited by Lester M. Salamon (Oxford University Press, 2002), pp. 1–47.
For specific discussions of such tools as loan guarantees, tax expenditures, and
vouchers, see chapters 6, 7, and 8, respectively, of that volume.

16. Even this understates the change, since, as noted below, most states have
taken advantage of the option provided in the Child Care and Development Block
Grant law to deliver block grant assistance in the form of vouchers. Data on tax
expenditures for child care are from U.S. Office of Management and Budget, *Ana-
lytical Perspectives, Budget of the U.S. Government, FY2016* (www.whitehouse.gov
/omb/budget/Analytical_Perspectives), p. 225; information on the Child Care
and Development Block Grant is from U.S. Office of Management and Budget,
Budget of the U.S. Government for Fiscal Year 2016, p. 489 (www.whitehouse.gov
/omb/budget).

17. Salamon, *Partners in Public Service,* p. 208. Both Medicare and Medicaid
are essentially voucher programs since consumers are entitled to choose their provider and the government then reimburses the provider. Spending on Medicaid,
for example, swelled more than fourfold in real dollar terms between 1975 and
1998, while discretionary spending stagnated or declined. Computed from data in
House Committee on Ways and Means, *2000 Green Book,* pp. 912, 923.

18. House Committee on Ways and Means, *2000 Green Book,* pp. 599, 617, 912, 923.

19. Of these, 40 percent of employees of large establishments and 35 percent of employees of small establishments were covered by preferred provider plans; the balance were covered by true HMOs. U.S. Census Bureau, *Statistical Abstract of the United States: 2000,* table 180 (Washington: U.S. Census Bureau, 2000).

20. For further detail on how these pressures have affected nonprofit organizations, see Salamon, ed., *The State of Nonprofit America,* particularly chapters 2, 3, 4, and 5 on health, education, social welfare, and the arts, respectively. For an interesting analysis of the pressures on nonprofits to find new market niches, see Peter Frumkin and Alice Andre-Clark, "When Missions, Markets, and Politics Collide: Values and Strategy in the Nonprofit Human Services," *Nonprofit and Voluntary Sector Quarterly* 29, no. 1 (2000), S141–63.

21. For detail on this latter point, see Mark Chaves, "Religious Congregations," in *The State of Nonprofit America,* edited by Salamon, pp. 379–87.

22. Author's estimates based on data in Murray S. Weitzman et al., *The New Nonprofit Almanac and Desk Reference, 2002* (San Francisco: Jossey-Bass, 2002), pp. 96–97.

23. Computed from data in ibid., pp. 96–97. For further discussion of trends in private giving, see Eleanor Brown and David Martin, "Individual Giving and Volunteering," in *The State of Nonprofit America,* edited by Salamon, pp. 495–520. Data on giving to religious congregations here are based on Giving USA Foundation, *Giving USA, 2009* (Indianapolis: Giving USA Foundation, 2009), p. 214.

24. Sources of data on the growth of private giving and overall revenue of nonprofit service and expressive organizations for 1997 and 2007 are from Lester M. Salamon, *America's Nonprofit Sector: A Primer,* 3rd ed. (New York: Foundation Center, 2012), chapter 3, n. 18. Data on the 2007–11 period are from Internal Revenue Service Statistics of Income Microdata Files, Internal Revenue Service, "SOI Tax Stats—Charities and Other Tax-Exempt Organizations Statistics" (www.irs.gov/uac/SOI-Tax-Stats-Charities-and-Other-Tax-Exempt-Organizations-Statistics) [accessed December 2014].

25. Based on data in U.S. Census Bureau, *Economic Census, 1999* (Washington: U.S. Census Bureau, 2000); U.S. Department of Education, *Digest of Education Statistics, 2000* (Washington: Department of Education, 2001), pp. 209, 202–03.

26. U.S. Bureau of the Census, *Economic Census, 1997* (Washington: Bureau of the Census, 1998); U.S. Bureau of the Census, *Economic Census, 2012* (Washington: Bureau of the Census, 2013).

27. Frumkin and Andre-Clark, "When Missions, Markets, and Politics Collide."

28. U.S. Department of Education, *Digest of Education Statistics, 1981* (Washington: Department of Education, 1982); U.S. Department of Education, *Digest of Education Statistics, 2007* (Washington: Department of Education, 2008).

29. The Fidelity Gift Fund recorded assets of $2.2 billion as of early 2000 and made grants of $374 million in the 1998–99 fiscal year. By comparison, the New York Community Trust reported assets of $2 billion as of the end of 1999 and grants during 1999 of $130.7 million. *Giving USA, 2001* (Indianapolis: AAFRC Trust for Philanthropy, 2001), p. 53; Foundation Center, *Foundation Yearbook, 2001* (New York: Foundation Center, 2002), pp. 67–68. For further insight into the growth of corporate-originated charitable gift funds, see Rick Cohen, "Corporate-Originated Charitable Funds," in *New Frontiers of Philanthropy: The New Actors and Tools Reshaping Global Philanthropy and Social Investment,* edited by Lester M. Salamon (Oxford University Press, 2014), pp. 255–90.

30. Andrew W. Hastings, ed., "Donor Advised Fund Market" (Jenkintown, Pa.: National Philanthropic Trust, 2008) (www.nptrust.org/images/Generic/DAF _White_Paper_12.03.08).

31. Lester M. Salamon and Stephanie L. Geller, "Investment Capital: The New Challenge for American Nonprofits," Listening Post Project Communiqué No. 5 (Baltimore: Center for Civil Society Studies, Johns Hopkins University, 2006) (http://ccss.jhu.edu/publications-findings/?did=265).

32. For a discussion of these efforts, see Lester M. Salamon, ed., *New Frontiers of Philanthropy: The New Actors and Tools Reshaping Global Philanthropy and Social Investment* (Oxford University Press, 2014); and Lester M. Salamon, *Leverage for Good: An Introduction to the New Frontiers of Philanthropy and Social Investment* (Oxford University Press, 2014).

33. William P. Ryan, "The New Landscape for Nonprofits," *Harvard Business Review* 77 (January/February 1999), p. 128.

34. Henry Hansmann, "The Role of Nonprofit Enterprise," *Yale Law Journal* 89, no. 5 (1980), pp. 835–901.

35. See, for example, Paul Brest and Hal Harvey, *Money Well Spent: A Strategic Plan for Smart Philanthropy* (New York: Bloomberg Press, 2008); Michael Porter and Mark R. Kramer, "Philanthropy's New Agenda: Creating Value," *Harvard Business Review* 77 (November/December 1999), pp. 121–30; Gar Walker and Jean Grossman, "Philanthropy and Outcomes," in *Philanthropy and the Nonprofit Sector in a Changing America,* edited by Charles Clotfelter and Thomas Ehrlich (Indiana University Press, 1999), pp. 449–60.

36. Christine W. Letts, William Ryan, and Allen Grossman, "Virtuous Capital: What Foundations Can Learn from Venture Capitalists," *Harvard Business Review* 75 (March/April 1997), pp. 2–7.

37. See, for example, Matthew Bishop and Michael Green, *Philanthrocapitalism: How the Rich Can Save the World* (New York: Bloomsbury Press, 2008); and Mario Morino, *Leap of Faith: Managing to Results in an Era of Scarcity* (Washington: Venture Philanthropy Partners, 2010) (www.vppartners.org/sites/default/files /documents/LOR_Full_Version_Facing_Pages.pdf).

38. See, for example, Kevin P. Kearns, "Accountability in the Nonprofit Sector," in *The State of Nonprofit America,* edited by Salamon, pp. 587–615.

39. H. George Frederickson, "First, There's Theory, Then, There's Practice," *Foundation News and Commentary* (March/April 2001), p. 38. See also Doug Easterling, "Using Outcome Evaluation to Guide Grant Making: Theory, Reality, and Possibilities," *Nonprofit and Voluntary Sector Quarterly* 29, no. 3 (2000), pp. 482–86; Walker and Grossman, "Philanthropy and Outcomes."

40. Andrew Blau, "More than Bit Players: How Information Technology Will Change the Ways Nonprofits and Foundations Work and Thrive in the Information Age," a report to the Surdna Foundation (New York: Surdna Foundation, 2001), p. 10.

41. Stephen Greene, "Astride the Digital Divide: Many Charities Struggle to Make Effective Use of New Technology," *Chronicle of Philanthropy,* January 11, 2001 (http://philanthropy.com/article/Astride-the-Digital-Divide/54079/).

42. Blau, "More than Bit Players," p. 9.

43. Stephanie Geller, Alan J. Abramson, and Erwin de Leon, "The Nonprofit Technology Gap: Myth or Reality," Listening Post Project Communiqué No. 20 (Baltimore: Center for Civil Society Studies, Johns Hopkins University, 2010) (http://ccss.jhu.edu/publications-findings/?did=246).

44. Stefan Toepler and Margaret J. Wyszomirki, "Arts and Culture," in *The State of Nonprofit America,* edited by Salamon, pp. 256–58.

45. Edwin Feulner, "Truth in Testimony," *Heritage Foundation Testimony,* August 22, 1996 (www.heritage.org/research/commentary/1996/08/truth-in-testimony).

46. Capital Research Center, "Our Mission" (http://capitalresearch.org/).

47. Kimberly Dennis, "Charities on the Dole," *Policy Review: Journal of American Citizenship* 76, no. 5 (1996), p. 5.

48. See, for example, Lisbeth Schorr, *Within Our Reach: Breaking the Cycle of Disadvantage* (New York: Anchor Books, 1988).

49. See, for example, Charles Murray, *Losing Ground: American Social Policy, 1950–1980* (New York: Basic Books, 1984).

50. For a discussion of the social enterprise phenomenon, see Dennis Young, Lester M. Salamon, and Mary Clark Grinsfelder, "Commercialization, Social Ventures, and For-Profit Competition," in *The State of Nonprofit America,* edited by Salamon, pp. 521–48; and David Bornstein, *How to Change the World: Social Entrepreneurs and the Power of New Ideas* (Oxford University Press, 2004). For examples of social ventures, see "Models and Best Practices: Social Enterprise," Community-Wealth.org (www.community-wealth.org/strategies/panel/social/models.html). For a discussion of the broader array of financial instruments and institutions supporting this development, see Salamon, *New Frontiers of Philanthropy.* For a conceptualization of this development as a fourth sector, see Heerad Sabeti and

the Fourth Sector Network Concept Working Group, "The Emerging Fourth Sector," executive summary (Washington: Aspen Institute, 2009). For an analysis of proposed new legal forms for the emerging social enterprise sector, see Marc Lane, *Social Enterprise: Empowering Mission-Driven Entrepreneurs* (Chicago: American Bar Association, 2011).

51. Roy Lubove, *The Professional Altruist: The Emergence of Social Work as a Career, 1880–1930* (Harvard University Press, 1965).

52. John McKnight, *The Careless Society: Community and Its Counterfeit* (New York: Basic Books, 1995), p. 10.

53. Stuart Butler, *Privatizing Federal Spending* (New York: Universe Books, 1985); Martin Anderson, *Imposters in the Temple: American Intellectuals Are Destroying Our Universities and Cheating Our Students* (Englewood Cliffs, N.J.: Simon and Schuster, 1992).

54. Regina Herzlinger, "Can Public Trust in Nonprofits and Governments Be Restored?" *Harvard Business Review* 74 (March/April 1996), p. 96.

55. Joel Fleischman, "To Merit and Preserve the Public's Trust in Not-For-Profit Organizations: The Urgent Need for New Strategies for Regulatory Reform," in *Philanthropy and the Nonprofit Sector in a Changing America,* edited by Clotfelter and Ehrlich, pp. 172–97. For a recent congressional challenge to the accountability features of nonprofits, see U.S. Senate Finance Committee, "Staff Document on Regulation on Tax-Exempt Organizations," June 22, 2004.

56. Independent Sector, *Giving and Volunteering, 1999* (Washington: Independent Sector, 1999), pp. 3, 5.

57. "While a third of adults think the nonprofit sector in the United States is headed in the wrong direction, a vast majority of households have donated to charities in the past year." Harris Poll 33, April 27, 2006 (www.harrisinteractive .com/harris_poll/printerfriend/index.asp?PID=657). See also Paul C. Light, "How Americans View Charities: A Report on Charitable Confidence, 2008," *Issues in Governance Studies* 13 (Brookings, 2008). For an alternative view emphasizing Americans' continued willingness to make charitable contributions, see Michael C. O'Neill, "Public Confidence in Charitable Nonprofits," *Nonprofit and Voluntary Sector Quarterly* 38, no. 2 (2009), pp. 237–69.

58. Michael Cooper, "Squeezed Cities Ask Nonprofits for More Money," *New York Times,* May 12, 2011, p. A1 (www.nytimes.com/2011/05/12/us/12non profits.html).

59. Lester M. Salamon, Stephanie L. Geller, and S. Wojciech Sokolowski, "Taxing the Tax-Exempt Sector: A Growing Danger for Nonprofit Organizations," Listening Post Project Communiqué No. 21 (Baltimore: Center for Civil Society Studies, Johns Hopkins University, 2011) (http://ccss.jhu.edu/publications -findings/?did=244).

60. Adam Liptak, "Justices, 5-4, Reject Corporate Spending Limit," *New York Times,* January 21, 2010, p. A1 (www.nytimes.com/2010/01/22/us/politics/22 scotus.html).

61. Bruce R. Hopkins, *The Law of Tax-Exempt Organizations,* 9th ed. (New York: Wiley, 2007), p. 381. On the role of the 1969 restriction on foundation financing efforts to influence legislation as a penalty for foundation support of the civil rights movement in the South, see Oliver Zunz, *Philanthropy in America: A History* (Princeton University Press, 2012), pp. 201–31.

62. Gail Harmon, Diane Curran, and Anne Spielberg, "Regulation of Advocacy Activities for Nonprofits that Receive Federal Grants" (Washington: Alliance for Justice, n.d.).

63. See, for example, Peggy Gavin and Deanna Gelak, "Lobbying Disclosure Databases: A User's Guide," *Online* 32, no. 5 (2008), pp. 34–38; Campaign Finance Institute, "Fast Start for Soft Money Groups in 2008 Election: 527s Adapt to New Rules, 501(c)(4)s on the Upswing" (Washington: Campaign Finance Institute, 2008).

64. Phillip Howe and Corinne McDonald, "Traumatic Stress, Turnover, and Peer Support in Child Welfare" (Washington: Child Welfare League of America) (http://66.227.70.18/programs/trieschman/2001fbwPhilHowe.htm).

65. Abby Stoddard, "International Assistance," in *The State of Nonprofit America,* edited by Salamon, pp. 343–45.

66. Alicia Schoshinski, "Retention Challenges and Solutions for Nonprofits," Nonprofit HR, June 6, 2013 (www.nonprofithr.com/retention-challenges-and -solutions-for-nonprofits).

67. Paul Light, *Making Nonprofits Work: A Report on the Tides of Nonprofit Management Reform* (Brookings, 2000), p. 10. Among public policy program graduates in the classes of 1973, 1974, 1978, and 1979, an average of 14 percent took their first jobs in the nonprofit sector and 14 percent remained employed in the nonprofit sector in the mid-1990s. By contrast, an average of 16 percent of these graduates took their first job in the private business sector, and 33 percent were employed in the business sector as of the mid-1990s.

68. Jeanne Peters and Timothy Wolfred, *Daring to Lead: Nonprofit Executive Directors and Their Work Experience* (San Francisco: CompassPoint, 2001), pp. 13–14, 20–21.

69. Toepler and Wyszomirski, "Arts and Culture."

Chapter 5

1. U.S. Census Bureau, *Statistical Abstract of the United States, 2011* (Washington: Census Bureau, 2012), table 8.

2. Atul Dighe, "Demographic and Technological Imperatives," in *The State of Nonprofit America,* 2nd ed., edited by Lester M. Salamon (Brookings, 2012), pp. 616–39.

3. U.S. Census Bureau, *Statistical Abstract of the United States, 2000* (Washington: Census Bureau, 2012), pp. 408–09; *Statistical Abstract of the United States, 2011,* table 598.

4. *Statistical Abstract of the United States, 2000*, p. 71; *Statistical Abstract of the United States, 2011,* tables 129, 85.

5. U.S. Bureau of the Census, *Statistical Abstract of the United States, 1983* (Washington: Bureau of the Census, 1984), table 197; *Statistical Abstract of the United States, 2011,* table 202.

6. *Statistical Abstract of the United States, 2011,* table 43.

7. Paul Ray and Sherry Ruth Anderson, *Cultural Creatives: How 50 Million People Are Changing the World* (San Francisco: Harmony Press, 2000).

8. Neil Gilbert, "The Transformation of Social Services," *Social Services Review* 51, no. 4 (1977), pp. 624–41.

9. For a statement of the importance of social capital and the nonprofit sector's contribution to it, see Robert Putnam, *Making Democracy Work: Civic Traditions in Modern Italy* (Princeton University Press, 1993), pp. 163–86.

10. Roseanne Mirabella, "Nonprofit Management Education: Current Offerings in University-Based Programs," Seton Hall University blog (http://academic.shu.edu/npo/). See also Roseanne Mirabella, "University-Based Educational Programs in Nonprofit Management and Philanthropic Studies: A 10-Year Review and Projections of Future Trends," *Nonprofit and Voluntary Sector Quarterly* 36, no. 4 (2007), pp. S11–S27.

11. For a discussion of the competing evidence on public confidence in nonprofit organizations, see Michael C. O'Neill, "Public Confidence in Charitable Nonprofits," *Nonprofit and Voluntary Sector Quarterly* 38, no. 2 (2009), pp. 237–69.

12. See, for example, Alan J. Abramson and Rachel McCarthy, "Infrastructure Organizations," in *The State of Nonprofit America,* edited by Salamon, pp. 423–58.

13. Dighe, "Demographic and Technological Imperatives," pp. 617–24.

14. John J. Havens and Paul G. Schervish, "Millionaires and the Millennium: New Estimates of the Forthcoming Wealth Transfer and the Prospects for a Golden Age of Philanthropy" (Social Welfare Research Institute, Boston College, 1999).

15. Craig Smith, "The New Corporate Philanthropy," *Harvard Business Review* 72 (May/June 1994), pp. 105–16; Jane Nelson, *Business as Partners in Development: Creating Wealth for Countries, Companies, and Communities* (London: Prince of Wales Business Leaders Forum, 1996); Lester M. Salamon, *Rethinking Corporate Social Engagement: Lessons from Latin America* (Sterling, Va.: Kumarian Press, 2010).

16. Matthew Bishop and Michael Green, *Philanthrocapitalism: How the Rich Can Save the World* (New York: Bloomsbury Press, 2008).

17. *New Frontiers of Philanthropy: The New Actors and Tools Reshaping Global Philanthropy and Social Investment*, edited by Lester M. Salamon (Oxford University Press, 2014); Antony Bugg-Levine and Jed Emerson, *Impact Investing: Transforming How We Make Money while Making a Difference* (San Francisco: Jossey-Bass, 2011).

Chapter 6

1. Rosabeth Moss Kanter and David V. Summers, "Doing Well while Doing Good: Dilemmas of Performance Management in Nonprofit Organizations and the Need for a Multiple-Constituency Approach," in *The Nonprofit Sector: A Research Handbook*, edited by Walter W. Powell (Yale University Press, 1987), p. 154.

2. Regina Herzlinger, "Can Public Trust in Nonprofits and Governments Be Restored?" *Harvard Business Review* 74 (March/April 1996), p. 98.

3. Estimates of nonprofit revenue in this section are drawn from two broad sets of sources. For the period 1977–96, author's estimates are based on data in Virginia Hodgkinson et al., *Nonprofit Almanac, Dimensions of the Independent Sector, 1996–1997* (Washington: Independent Sector, 1997), pp. 190–91; on unpublished data supplied by Independent Sector; and on U.S. Bureau of the Census, *Service Annual Survey, 1996* (www.census.gov/services/sas/historic data .html). For these estimates, social and fraternal organizations are deleted from the broader category of "civic, social, and fraternal organizations" with which they are grouped in the economic census data, and social services are grouped with the remaining civic organizations. Inflation adjustment is based on the implicit price deflator for the services component of personal consumption expenditures as reported in the *Economic Report of the President* (February 1998), p. 290. For the period 1997–2007, estimates were developed from special tabulations available from the Internal Revenue Service, Statistics of Income, supplemented by data from the U.S. Census Bureau, *Service Annual Survey, 2006* (www.census.gov/services /sas/historic_data.html), on government voucher payments (Medicare and Medicaid) to nonprofit organizations. For the 2007–11 data, estimates were developed from IRS Statistics of Income microdata for 2007 and 2011. GDP data were secured from the Bureau of Economic Analysis (BEA) National Income and Product Account (NIPA) table 1.3.6. Inflation adjustment was based on NIPA table 1.9.4. Despite adjustments to reported nonprofit "program service revenue" on Form 990 records to correct the problem, the fee portion of nonprofit revenue may still be overstated somewhat due to the fact that government contract and voucher pay-

ments are treated as program service revenue on Form 990 (filed by nonprofits and used by the Internal Revenue Service in its data). For further detail, see Lester M. Salamon, *America's Nonprofit Sector: A Primer,* 3rd ed. (New York: Foundation Center, 2012), chapter 3, n. 18.

4. Based on Lester M. Salamon, *America's Nonprofit Sector,* 2nd ed. (New York: Foundation Center, 2009), p. 68.

5. U.S. Internal Revenue Service, *Data Book,* various years (recent editions accessed at www.irs.gov/uac/SOI-Tax-Stats-IRS-Data-Book). Nonprofit organizations are not required to incorporate or register with the Internal Revenue Service unless they have annual gross receipts of $5,000 or more and wish to avail themselves of the charitable tax exemption. Religious congregations are not required to register even if they exceed these limits, though many do. It is therefore likely that more organizations exist than are captured in IRS records. It is also possible, however, that some of the new registrants are organizations that have long existed but have chosen to register only in recent years. Because the legal and financial advantages of registration are substantial, however, it seems likely that the data reported here represent real growth in the number of organizations despite these caveats.

6. This same picture of organizational vitality emerges as well from detailed scrutiny of the Form 990 that registered nonprofit organizations are obliged to file with the Internal Revenue Service. Because these forms are only required of organizations with $25,000 or more in revenue, it might be assumed that older and larger organizations would dominate the reporting agencies. Yet a recent analysis of these reporting organizations reveals that about half of those in existence as of 2005 had been founded since 1992, though among organizations with at least $5 million in expenditures, this was true of fewer than one-quarter of the organizations. Kennard T. Wing, Thomas H. Pollack, and Amy Blackwood, *The Nonprofit Almanac, 2008* (Washington: Urban Institute, 2008), p. 143.

7. This phenomenon was already apparent in the early 1990s. See, for example, Lester M. Salamon, "The Marketization of Welfare: Changing Nonprofit and For-Profit Roles in the American Welfare State," *Social Service Review* 67, no. 1 (1993), pp. 17–39.

8. On the growth of religious congregation commercial income, see Mark Chaves, "Religious Congregations," in *The State of Nonprofit America,* 2nd ed., edited by Lester M. Salamon (Brookings, 2012), pp. 372–76.

9. Julian Wolpert, *Patterns of Generosity in America: Who's Holding the Safety Net?* (New York: Twentieth Century Fund, 1993), pp. 7, 27, 39–40; Sarah Dewees and Lester M. Salamon, "Maryland Nonprofit Employment Update," Nonprofit Economic Data Bulletin No. 9 (Baltimore: Center for Civil Society Studies, Johns Hopkins University, 2002) (http://ccss.jhu.edu/publications-findings/?did =296).

10. Lester M. Salamon and Wojciech Sokolowski, "Nonprofits and Recession: New Data from Maryland," *Nonprofit Economic Data Bulletin No. 33* (Baltimore: Center for Civil Society Studies, Johns Hopkins University, 2011) (http://ccss.jhu.edu/publications-findings/?did=289).

11. On this point, see Avis C. Vidal, "Housing and Community Development," in *The State of Nonprofit America,* edited by Salamon, pp. 285–86.

12. See, for example, Raymond Hernandez, "A Broad Alliance Tries to Head off Cuts in Medicare," *New York Times,* May 13, 2001, p. A1 (www.nytimes .com/2001/05/14/nyregion/a-broad-alliance-tries-to-head-off-cuts-in-medicare .html).

13. Harvey Lipman and Elizabeth Schwinn, "The Business of Charity: Nonprofit Groups Reap Billions in Tax-Free Income Annually," *Chronicle of Philanthropy,* October 18, 2001, p. 25 (http://philanthropy.com/article/The-Business-of -Charity/52259/).

14. Margaret Riley, "Unrelated Business Income of Nonprofit Organizations, 1997," *IRS Statistics of Income Bulletin* (2008), p. 125; Jael Jackson, "Unrelated Business Income Tax Returns, 2007," *IRS Statistics of Income Bulletin* (Washington: Internal Revenue Service, 2008), p. 154. The number of 501(c)(3) charities filing unrelated business income returns grew by another 12 percent between 2007 and 2011, and the amount of unrelated business income they reported grew by nearly 10 percent. At the same time, the taxes paid on such income declined from $277 million to $199 million. U.S. IRS, "SOI Tax Stats—Exempt Organizations' Unrelated Business Income (UBI) Tax Statistics," 2007 and 2011 (www.irs.gov /uac/SOI-Tax-Stats-Exempt-Organizations'-Unrelated-Business-Income-UBI-Tax -Statistics) [accessed March 20, 2014].

15. For a discussion of this facet of nonprofit arts organization activity, see Stefan Toepler and Margaret J. Wyszomirki, "Arts and Culture," in *The State of Nonprofit America,* edited by Salamon, pp. 251–53.

16. Melena Ryzik, "Ideas for Sale by Museums and Artists: Poof! At the Walker, Evanescent New Ways to Blur Creativity and Commerce," *New York Times,* March 19, 2015, p. F1 (www.nytimes.com/2015/03/19/arts/artsspecial/for-the-walker -art-center-a-shop-that-peddles-evanescence.html).

17. On the latter, see the website of FEI Behavioral Health, a subsidiary of Families International, a holding company for an association of nonprofit family and children service organizations, at www.feinet.com.

18. See, for example, Mary Williams Walsh, "Hospital Group's Link to Company Is Criticized," *New York Times,* April 27, 2002, p. B1 (www.nytimes.com/2002/04 /27/business/hospital-group-s-link-to-company-is-criticized.html); Walt Bogdanich, "Two Hospital Fundraising Groups Face Questions over Conflicts," *New York Times,* March 24, 2002, p. A1.

19. This conception of social enterprises follows the definition used by the Social Enterprise Alliance: a social enterprise is an organization that achieves its primary social or environmental purpose through a business. Other definitions of social enterprises are not this demanding. For a discussion of the alternative definitions of social enterprises, see Marc Lane, *Social Enterprise: Empowering Mission-Driven Entrepreneurs* (Chicago: American Bar Association, 2011), pp. 3–7.

20. Roberts Enterprise Development Fund, *Social Purpose Enterprises and Venture Philanthropy in the New Millennium* (San Francisco: REDF, 1999). For other examples of social enterprises, see Lane, *Social Enterprise,* pp. 1–2; and "Models and Best Practices: Social Enterprise," Community-Wealth.org (www.community-wealth.org/strategies/panel/social/models.html).

21. Lane, *Social Enterprise,* pp. 9–13; Stephanie Strom, "A Quest for Hybrid Companies That Profit, but Can Tap Charity," *New York Times,* October 13, 2011, p. B1 (www.nytimes.com/2011/10/13/business/a-quest-for-hybrid-companies-part-money-maker-part-nonprofit.html). In 2013, North Carolina became the first state to cancel its L3C law following opposition from lawyers who felt it added an unnecessary complexity to existing limited liability corporation laws (www.llclawmonitor.com/2013/07/articles/low-profit-llcs/north-carolina-becomes-the-first-state-to-drop-l3cs/).

22. David Bornstein, *How to Change the World: Social Entrepreneurs and the Power of New Ideas* (Oxford University Press, 2004); C. K. Prahalad, *The Fortune at the Bottom of the Pyramid: Eradicating Poverty through Profits,* rev. ed. (Philadelphia: Wharton School Publishing, 2010); and Stephen Goldsmith, *The Power of Social Innovation: How Civic Entrepreneurs Ignite Community Networks for Good* (San Francisco: Jossey-Bass, 2010).

23. The paid employment of public-benefit nonprofit organizations grew at an annual average rate of 3.3 percent between 1977 and 1994, compared to 1.9 percent for all nonagricultural employment. Bureau of Labor Statistics data as reported in Hodgkinson et al., *Nonprofit Almanac, 1996–1997,* p. 129.

24. Nonprofit employment grew by an estimated 16.4 percent between 1995 and 2008 while total nonfarm employment grew by only 6.2 percent. Wing, Pollack, and Blackwood, *Nonprofit Almanac, 2008,* table 1.8.

25. According to data secured from the Bureau of Labor Statistics' Quarterly Census of Employment and Wages, in the decade of 2000–2010, the nonprofit sector achieved an annual average employment growth rate of 2.1 percent compared to an annual average growth rate of minus 0.6 percent for employment in the for-profit sector. For further detail, see Lester M. Salamon, S. Wojciech Sokolowski, and Stephanie L. Geller, "Holding the Fort: Nonprofit Employment during a Decade of Turmoil," Nonprofit Economic Data Bulletin No. 38.

(Baltimore: Center for Civil Society Studies, Johns Hopkins University, 2012) (http://ccss.jhu.edu/publications-findings?did=369).

26. Joseph Horowitz, *Classical Music in America: A History of Its Rise and Fall* (New York: W. W. Norton, 2005), p. 534; Toepler and Wyszomirski, "Arts and Culture," pp. 249–51.

27. Peter Dobkin Hall, "Historical Perspectives on Nonprofit Organizations," in *The Jossey-Bass Handbook of Nonprofit Leadership and Management*, edited by Robert D. Herman (San Francisco: Jossey-Bass, 1994), p. 28.

28. Hokyu Hwang and Walter W. Powell, "The Rationalization of Charity: The Influences of Professionalism in the Nonprofit Sector," *Administrative Science Quarterly* 54, no. 2 (2009), pp. 286–92.

29. Kevin P. Kearns, *Private Sector Strategies for Social Sector Success: The Guide to Strategy and Planning for Public and Nonprofit Organizations* (San Francisco: Jossey-Bass, 2000), p. 25.

30. Lester M. Salamon, Stephanie L. Geller, and Kasey L. Mengel, "Nonprofits, Innovation, and Performance Measurement: Separating Fact from Fiction," Listening Post Project Communiqué No. 17, (Baltimore: Center for Civil Society Studies, Johns Hopkins University, 2010) (http://ccss.jhu.edu/publications -findings/?did=249).

31. Based on recent offerings from the John Wiley and Sons website (www .wiley.co.uk/products/subject/business/nonprofit/management.html).

32. Frances Hesselbein, "Foreword," in Peter Drucker, *The Drucker Foundation Self-Assessment Tool,* rev. ed. (San Francisco: Jossey-Bass, 1999), p. vi.

33. Hwang and Powell, "Rationalization of Charity," p. 288.

34. See "About AFP," AFP.org (www.afpnet.org/About/content.cfm?item number=619).

35. For an analysis of these corporate-initiated charitable funds, see Rick Cohen, "Corporate-Originated Charitable Funds," in *New Frontiers of Philanthropy: The New Actors and Tools Reshaping Global Philanthropy and Social Investment,* edited by Lester M. Salamon (Oxford University Press, 2014), pp. 255–90.

36. For an analysis of these new actors and new tools, see Salamon, *New Frontiers of Philanthropy.*

37. On this development, see Elizabeth Boris and Marrhew Maronick, "Civic Participation and Advocacy," in *The State of Nonprofit America,* edited by Salamon, pp. 408–19.

38. See, for example, Walter W. Powell and Jason Owen-Smith, "Universities as Creators and Retailers of Intellectual Property," in *To Profit or Not to Profit: The Commercial Transformation of the Nonprofit Sector,* edited by Burton A. Weisbrod (Cambridge University Press, 1998), pp. 169–93.

39. Roseanne Mirabella, "Nonprofit Management Education: Current Offerings in University-Based Programs," Seton Hall University blog (http://academic

.shu.edu/npo/); Roseanne Mirabella, "University-Based Educational Programs in Nonprofit Management and Philanthropic Studies: A 10-Year Review and Projections of Future Trends," *Nonprofit and Voluntary Sector Quarterly* 36, no. 4 (2007), pp. S11–S27.

40. On this development, see Alan J. Abramson and Rachel McCarthy, "Infrastructure Organizations," in *The State of Nonprofit America,* edited by Salamon, pp. 423–58.

41. Tracy Thompson, "Profit with Honor," *Washington Post Magazine,* December 19, 1999, pp. 7–22.

42. Susan Gray and Holly Hall, "Cashing in on Charity's Good Name," *Chronicle of Philanthropy,* July 20, 1998, p. 26 (http://philanthropy.com/article/Cashing-In-on-Charitys-Good/53390/); Cause Related Marketing, "Sponsorship Spending on Causes to Total $1.55 Billion This Year" (San Francisco: Business for Social Responsibility Education Fund, 1999) (www.sponsorship.com/IEGSR/2009/07/27/Sponsorship-Spending-On-Causes-To-Total-$1-55-Bill.aspx); "The Growth of Cause Marketing," Cause Marketing Forum (www.causemarketingforum.com/site/c.bkLUKcOTLkK4E/b.6452355/apps/s/content.asp?ct=8965443).

43. Eyal Press and Jennifer Washburn, "The Kept University," *Atlantic Monthly,* March 2000, pp. 39–40 (www.theatlantic.com/magazine/archive/2000/03/the-kept-university/306629).

44. Rosabeth Moss Kanter, "From Spare Change to Real Change: The Social Sector as Beta Site for Business Innovation," *Harvard Business Review* 77 (May/June 1999) (https://hbr.org/1999/05/from-spare-change-to-real-change-the-social-sector-as-beta-site-for-business-innovation).

45. Nonprofit Sector Strategy Group, "The Nonprofit Sector and Business: New Visions, New Opportunities, New Challenges" (Washington: Aspen Institute, 2001), p. 1.

46. On the "life-cycle" concept of competition in the health field, see Bradford H. Gray and Mark Schlesinger, "Health Care," in *The State of Nonprofit America,* edited by Salamon, pp. 89–136.

47. See, for example, Kurt Eichenwald, "Columbia/HCA Fraud Case May Be Widened, U.S. Says," *New York Times,* February 28, 1998 (www.nytimes.com/1998/02/14/business/columbia-hca-fraud-case-may-be-widened-us-says.html); and Reed Abelson and Julie Creswell, "Hospital Chain Inquiry Cited Unnecessary Cardiac Work," *New York Times,* August 7, 2012 (www.nytimes.com/2012/08/07/business/hospital-chain-internal-reports-found-dubious-cardiac-work.html).

48. For an interesting example of a nonprofit strategy for meeting the for-profit competition in the field of welfare services, see Peter Frumkin and Alice Andre-Clark, "When Missions, Markets, and Politics Collide: Values and Strategy in the Nonprofit Human Services," *Nonprofit and Voluntary Sector Quarterly* 29, no. 1 (2000), S141–63.

49. Arnold Relman, "How Doctors Could Rescue Health Care," *New York Review of Books,* October 27, 2011, p. 16 (www.nybooks.com/articles/archives/2011 /oct/27/how-doctors-could-rescue-health-care).

50. Since the beginning of 2000, Moody's Investors Service has downgraded the bonds of 121 nonprofit hospitals, affecting $24 billion in bonds. See Reed Abelson, "Demand, but No Capital, at Nonprofit Hospitals," *New York Times,* June 12, 2002, p. B1 (www.nytimes.com/2002/06/21/business/demand-but-no -capital-at-nonprofit-hospitals.html).

51. Robert D. Putnam, *Bowling Alone: The Collapse and Revival of American Community* (New York: Simon and Schuster, 2000); Theda Skocpol, *Diminished Democracy: From Membership to Management in American Civic Life* (Oklahoma University Press, 1987).

52. On the role of technology in facilitating nonprofit issue advocacy, see Atul Dighe, "Demographic and Technological Imperatives," in *The State of Nonprofit America,* edited by Salamon, pp. 623–24.

53. Jeffrey Berry, *The New Liberalism: The Rising Power of Citizen Groups* (Brookings, 1999).

54. For further detail on these and other citizen engagement activities, see Carmen Sirianni and Lewis Friedland, *Civic Innovation in America: Community Empowerment, Public Policy, and the Movement for Civic Renewal* (University of California Press, 2001); and Carmen Sirianni and Stephanie Sofer, "Environmental Organizations," in *The State of Nonprofit America,* edited by Salamon, pp. 294–328.

55. The National Audubon Society thus claims 600,000 members, the Natural Resources Defense Council, 564,000, and the Wilderness Society, 400,000.

56. Gary D. Bass, David F. Arons, Kay Guinane, and Matthew F. Carter, *Seen but Not Heard: Strengthening Nonprofit Advocacy* (Washington: Aspen Institute, 2007); Lester M. Salamon and Stephanie Lessans Geller, "Nonprofit America: A Force for Democracy?" Listening Post Project Communiqué No. 9, (Baltimore: Center for Civil Society Studies, Johns Hopkins University, 2008) (http://ccss.jhu .edu/publications-findings/?did=260).

57. As noted earlier in this volume, "lobbying" differs from "advocacy" in that it is directed at specific pieces of legislation. No limitations impede nonprofit involvement in advocacy activity. Only lobbying is restricted.

58. See, for example, Margaret E. Keck and Kathryn Sikkink, *Activists beyond Borders: Advocacy Networks in International Politics* (Cornell University Press, 1999); Anne M. Florini, ed., *The Third Force: The Rise of Transnational Civil Society* (Washington: Japan Center for International Exchange and the Carnegie Endowment for International Peace, 2000).

59. Salamon and Geller, "Nonprofit America: Force for Democracy?" This finding is wholly consistent with the prior Strengthening Nonprofit Advocacy Project (SNAP) findings. See Bass et al., *Seen but Not Heard*.

60. Salamon and Geller, "Nonprofit America: A Force for Democracy?"

61. Boris and Maronick, "Civic Participation and Advocacy," pp. 401–05.

62. Sirianni and Sofer, "Environmental Organizations," pp. 319–20.

63. Berry, *The New Liberalism*, p. 57.

64. Jacob S. Hacker and Paul Pierson, *Winner-Take-All Politics: How Washington Made the Rich Richer—And Turned Its Back on the Middle Class* (New York: Simon and Schuster, 2010), p. 147.

65. Ibid., pp. 118, 121.

Chapter 7

1. Bradford H. Gray and Mark Schlesinger, "Health Care," in *The State of Nonprofit America,* 2nd ed., edited by Lester M. Salamon (Brookings, 2012), pp. 105–06.

2. A classic statement of this tension, focusing on a much earlier period, can be found in David Rosner, *A Once Charitable Enterprise: Hospitals and Health Care in Brooklyn and New York, 1885–1915* (Cambridge University Press, 1982). For more recent analyses, see Regina Herzlinger and William S. Krasker, "Who Profits from Nonprofits?" *Harvard Business Review* 65 (January/February 1987), pp. 93–106; David S. Salkever and Richard G. Frank, "Health Services," in *Who Benefits from the Nonprofit Sector*, edited by Charles T. Clotfelter (University of Chicago Press, 1992), pp. 24–54.

3. Eyal Press and Jennifer Washburn, "The Kept University," *Atlantic Monthly,* March 2000, pp. 39–40 (www.theatlantic.com/magazine/archive/2000/03/the -kept-university/306629); Donald M. Stuart, Pearl Rock Kane, and Lisa Scruggs, "Education and Training," in *The State of Nonprofit America,* edited by Salamon, pp. 147–49.

4. Estelle James, "Commercialism among Nonprofits: Objectives, Opportunities, and Constraints," in *To Profit or Not to Profit: The Commercial Transformation of the Nonprofit Sector,* edited by Burton A. Weisbrod (Cambridge University Press, 1998), p. 273. For the alternative theory, see Burton A. Weisbrod, "Modeling the Nonprofit Organization as a Multiproduct Firm: A Framework for Choice," in *To Profit or Not to Profit,* edited by Weisbrod, pp. 47–64.

5. Evelyn Brody, "Agents without Principals: The Economic Convergence of the Nonprofit and For-Profit Organizational Forms," *New York Law School Law*

Review 40, no. 3 (1996), pp. 457–536. See also Salamon, ed., *The State of Nonprofit America,* chapter 16.

6. On some of these latter dangers associated with social-impact investment, see Lester M. Salamon, *Leverage for Good: Introduction to the New Frontiers of Philanthropy and Social Investment* (Oxford University Press, 2014), pp. 93–97.

7. For an interesting development of this line of argument, see Pascale Joassart-Marcelli, "For Whom and for What? Investigating the Role of Nonprofits as Providers to the Neediest," in *The State of Nonprofit America,* edited by Salamon, pp. 657–82.

8. James, "Commercialism among Nonprofits," p. 279.

9. Amelia Kohm, David La Piana, and Heather Gowdy, *Strategic Restructuring: Findings from a Study of Integrations and Alliances among Nonprofit Social Service and Cultural Organizations in the United States* (Chicago: Chapin Hall Center for Children, 2000).

10. For a discussion of the limitations on the social problem-solving role of U.S. congregations, see Mark Chaves, "Religious Congregations," in *The State of Nonprofit America,* edited by Salamon, pp. 379–87.

Chapter 8

1. I am indebted to Bradford Gray and Mark Schlesinger for articulating this distinction. See Bradford H. Gray and Mark Schlesinger, "Health Care," in *The State of Nonprofit America,* 2nd ed., edited by Lester M. Salamon (Brookings, 2012) pp. 123–27.

2. For examples of social ventures, see "Models and Best Practices: Social Enterprise," Community-Wealth.org (www.community-wealth.org/strategies/panel /social/models.html). For a discussion of the broader array of financial instruments and institutions supporting this development, see Lester M. Salamon, ed., *New Frontiers of Philanthropy: The New Actors and Tools Reshaping Global Philanthropy and Social Investment* (Oxford University Press, 2014). For a conceptualization of this development as a fourth sector, see Heerad Sabeti and the Fourth Sector Network Concept Working Group, "The Emerging Fourth Sector," executive summary (Washington: Aspen Institute, 2009).

3. Sam Daley-Harris, *State of the Microcredit Summit Campaign Report* (Washington: Microcredit Summit Campaign, 2009), p. 3.

4. See C. K. Prahalad, *The Fortune at the Bottom of the Pyramid: Eradicating Poverty through Profits,* rev. ed. (Philadelphia: Wharton School Publishing, 2010).

5. As John Gardner put it in his influential book on self-renewal, "Anyone concerned about the continuous renewal of society must be concerned for the renewal

of that society's values and beliefs." John Gardner, *Self-Renewal: The Individual and the Innovative Society,* rev. ed. (New York: W. W. Norton, 1981), p. 115.

6. The Listening Post Project is a collaborative undertaking of the Center for Civil Society Studies at the Johns Hopkins University Institute for Health and Social Policy, the Alliance for Children and Families, the Alliance for Nonprofit Management, the American Alliance of Museums, the Arc, Community Action Partnership, LeadingAge, the League of American Orchestras, Lutheran Services in America, the Michigan Nonprofit Association, the National Council of Non-profits, and United Neighborhood Centers of America. Its goal has been to monitor the health of the nation's nonprofit organizations and make nonprofit leaders and policymakers aware of issues of central importance to the sector and the people it serves.

7. A value proposition is a set of attributes or qualities thought to set a partic-ular organization or group of organizations apart from competing organizations or groups of organizations.

8. These results were reported in Lester M. Salamon, Stephanie L. Geller, and Chelsea L. Newhouse, "What Do Nonprofits Stand For? Renewing the Nonprofit Value Commitment," Listening Post Communiqué No. 22 (Baltimore: Center for Civil Society Studies, Johns Hopkins University, 2012) (http://ccss.jhu.edu /publications-findings/?did=389).

9. This term is drawn from the title of Lester M. Salamon, *Partners in Public Service: Government-Nonprofit Relations in the Modern Welfare State* (Johns Hop-kins University Press, 1995).

10. "Forward Together: Empowering America's Citizen Sector for the Change We Need," Center for Civil Society Studies, p. 2 (http://ccss.jhu.edu/publications -findings?did=322).

11. Avis C. Vidal, "Housing and Community Development," in *The State of Nonprofit America,* edited by Salamon, pp. 267–70. See also David J. Erickson, *The Housing Policy Revolution: Networks and Neighborhoods* (Washington: Urban Institute, 2009).

12. Lester M. Salamon, *Leverage for Good: An Introduction to the New Fron-tiers of Philanthropy and Social Investment* (Oxford University Press, 2014), pp. 97–99.

13. On the recent phenomenon of "foundations as philanthropic banks," see Lester M. Salamon and William Burckart, "Foundations as Philanthropic Banks," in *New Frontiers of Philanthropy,* edited by Salamon, pp. 165–209.

14. On this point, see U.S. National Advisory Board on Impact Investing, "Private Capital, Public Good: How Smart Federal Policy Can Galvanize Impact Investing—and Why It's Urgent," June 2014 (www.nabimpactinvesting.org/).

15. Under the existing tax deduction system, taxpayers are allowed to subtract their charitable contributions from their taxable income if they itemize their

deductions. Since higher-income taxpayers face higher tax rates, however, the resulting deductions are worth more to them than to lower-income taxpayers and those who do not itemize their deductions. Tax credits, however, are deducted from the actual taxes a taxpayer owes. Credits can be set equal to the contribution or at some fraction of the contribution (for example, 40 percent of the contribution can be deducted from the tax bill).

Index

40–43, 45, 84–85, 94, 109–10; tax credits for leveling, 109–10; voluntarism impacted by, 49

Cone/Roper survey on consumer attitudes toward corporate giving, 82

Conservative ideologies, 20, 34, 35, 37, 47; government-nonprofit partnership viewed by, 2–3

Consumer-side subsidies, 26, 35–38, 42, 71, 73

Contracts, government, 35

Contract with America, 33, 34

Conventional wisdom, about nonprofits, 63–64

Corporate partnerships. *See* Business partnerships

Corporate philanthropy, 60–61

Corporate structure, of nonprofits, 80–81

Council for Advancement and Support of Education, 79

Council on Foundations, 81

Cultural creatives, 57–58

Cultural subgroup demographics, 57–58

Culture. *See* Arts and culture

Daycare. *See* Child daycare services

Democracy in America (de Tocqueville), 16

Demographic trends, 3, 55; aging population, 56; cultural subgroup, 57–58; in family structure shifts, 56–57; immigration, 57; substance abuse, 57; women in labor force, 56

Deregulation, of advocacy and lobbying, 108

Digital divide, 45, 96

Distinctiveness imperative, 4, 27, 92, 99–100, 102, 112

Distributed learning, 60

Divorce rate, 56–57

Donor-advised funds, 41–42

Dot-com philanthropy, 44, 61, 101

Drucker Foundation's Self-Assessment Tool, 79

Drug and alcohol abuse treatment, 57

Earned income. *See* Revenues

Economic recovery program of *2009*, 34

Education, 1; commercial and technological dilemmas of, 46; commercial income in, 68; distributed learning, 60; 501(c)(3) status of, 8; for-profit and nonprofit market shares of, 41; revenues of, 10–11, 64–67, 70; service function of, 14–15

Effectiveness, 103, 104, 105, 106. *See also* Accountability

Employment, by nonprofits, 9, 10, 17, 40–41, 126n67; for-profit compared to, 77; human resource challenges of, 52–53. *See also* Staff

Empowerment, as nonprofit value, 102, 103, 104–06, 108

Encore careers, 56

Enrichment, as nonprofit value, 103, 104, 105, 106, 108

Entitlement programs: expansion of, 32–33; reduction of, 29, 34–35, 49; revenues from, 26, 70, 120n8

Entrepreneurs, social, 26–27, 59, 61, 76

Entrepreneurship, of nonprofits, 26, 78

Environmental activism, 87

E-philanthropy, 45–46, 79, 110

Expressive organizations: revenues of, 10–11, 12–13; sector size of, 9; types of, 15

Performance and outcome
measurements, 26, 44, 78, 102
Personal Responsibility and Work
Opportunity Reconciliation Act of
1996, 33
Philanthropy: accountability
requirements of, 43–44; business
ventures as, 75–76; corporate
collaboration in, 60–61; of dot-
coms, 44, 61, 101; E-philanthropy
in, 45–46, 79, 110; foundations as
philanthropic banks for, 43, 110;
fundraising organizations for,
79–80; intergenerational transfer
of wealth in, 60; opportunities in
new, 60–61; private giving declines
in, 38–39, 70; private investment
capital as, 80, 108–09; revenue
from, 12–13, 38–40, 70, 71; of
social entrepreneurs, 26–27, 59,
61, 76; of social investors, 61;
suburbanization of, 69; technology
impacting, 79
Pierson, Paul, 90
Pioneer Human Services, 75–76
Political action committees (PACs),
90
Political ideologies, 2–3, 58–59
Private giving, 38–39, 70
Private investment capital, 80, 101,
108–09
Productiveness, as nonprofit value,
103, 104–05, 107
Professionalism: of advocacy
function, 86, 87; of boards, 80;
of corporate structures, 80–81;
defined, 22, 117n4; government
involvement and, 22–23, 117n6; as
impulse shaping nonprofits, 1–2,
19–20, 21, 22–24; managerial,
76–81; overprofessionalism in,

49–50; performance metrics
as, 78; services strategy of, 48–49;
of social services, 77; of staffing,
23, 76–77; subject-matter
compared to managerial, 77–78,
117n4
Programmatic critique, of nonprofits,
47–49
Publications and journals, 76, 78–79,
81
Public attitudes, 3, 59; legitimacy
challenges in, 46–52; of nonprofit
trustworthiness, 43, 46, 64, 94, 97;
renewal by improving, 111; as risk
to nonprofits, 97
Public funding. *See* Government
support
Public policy influence, of nonprofits,
24, 87
Public-serving organizations:
employment by, 9, 10, 17, 40–41,
126n67; lobbying by, 9; revenues of,
9–13; sector size of, 9–12; tax
exempt status of, 8
Putnam, Robert, 86

Reagan administration, 32–33,
52, 59
Red Cross, 51
Reference groups, 19, 21, 22, 23–24,
25, 26, 95
Reimbursement rates: of Medicaid,
72–73, 84; of Medicare, 37, 42–43,
72, 84, 94, 108
Reliability, as nonprofit value, 103,
104, 105, 108
Religious organizations, 7, 15;
commercial income in, 68–69;
501(c)(3) status of, 8, 115n3;
revenues of, 10; sector size of, 9;
voluntarism of, 20